GAY AND LESBIAN WRITERS

Allen Ginsberg

GAY AND LESBIAN WRITERS

James Baldwin

Allen Ginsberg

Adrienne Rich

Sappho

Walt Whitman

Oscar Wilde

GAY AND LESBIAN WRITERS

Allen Ginsberg

Neil Heims

Lesléa Newman
Series Editor

CHELSEA HOUSE
PUBLISHERS
A Haights Cross Communications Company ®

Philadelphia

CHELSEA HOUSE PUBLISHERS

VP, NEW PRODUCT DEVELOPMENT Sally Cheney
DIRECTOR OF PRODUCTION Kim Shinners
CREATIVE MANAGER Takeshi Takahashi
MANUFACTURING MANAGER Diann Grasse

Staff for ALLEN GINSBERG

EXECUTIVE EDITOR: Matt Uhler
EDITORIAL ASSISTANT: Sarah Sharpless
PHOTO EDITOR: Sarah Bloom
SERIES AND COVER DESIGNER: Takeshi Takahashi
LAYOUT: EJB Publishing Services

http://www.chelseahouse.com

First Printing

9 8 7 6 5 4 3 2 1

Library of Congress Cataloging-in-Publication Data
Heims, Neil.
  Allen Ginsberg / Neil Heims.
     p. cm. — (Gay and lesbian writers)
  Includes bibliographical references.
  ISBN 0-7910-8224-5 (alk. paper)
  1. Ginsberg, Allen, 1926- 2. Poets, American—20th century—Biography. 3.
Gay men—United States—Biography. 4. Beat generation—Biography. I. Title.
II. Series.
  PS3513.I74Z618 2005
  811'.54—dc22

Cover: © Bettman/Corbis

All links and web addresses were checked and verified to be correct at
the time of publication. Because of the dynamic nature of the web,
some addresses and links may have changed since publication and may
no longer be valid.

TABLE OF CONTENTS

PRIDE

MANY YEARS AGO, IN 1970 to be exact, I began my career as a high school student. Those were the dark ages, before cell phones and CD players, before computers and cable TV, before the words "gay" and "pride" ever—at least to my knowledge—appeared in the same sentence. In fact, I remember the very first time I saw the word "gay" appear in a newspaper. It was in the early 1970s, a year after the 1969 Stonewall riots when a group of butches and drag queens fought back against a police raid on a gay bar, sparking what was then known as the "gay liberation movement." I was sitting in our Long Island living room with my brothers, my parents, and some visiting relatives. One of the adults picked up the newspaper, read a headline about the anniversary of Stonewall and said in a voice dripping with disapproval, "Well, all I can say is *gay* certainly meant something different in my time." There were a few murmurs of agreement, and then the matter was dropped. I learned very quickly that this subject was taboo in the Newman household.

Not that I had any inkling that I would grow up to be a lesbian. All I knew was that I didn't want to get married and have children, I wasn't interested in boys, and all I wanted to do was read books, write poetry, and spend time with my best friend, Vicki, who lived three houses away. My friendship with Vicki was strictly platonic, but even so, taunts of "Leslie the lezzie, Leslie the lezzie" followed me up and down the hallways of

Jericho High School. (I changed my name from Leslie to Lesléa when I was sixteen largely because, due to my gender-free name, I was, much to my horror, enrolled in the boys' gym class.)

Interestingly enough, Vicki was never once teased for being a lesbian; did my classmates know something I didn't know?

In 1973 I left home to attend the University of Vermont. There was no gay/straight alliance on campus, nor were there courses in gay literature or gay history. Though I studied the poetry of Gertrude Stein, I was never led to believe that Alice B. Toklas was anything more than the poet's housekeeper and cook. Though I studied Walt Whitman's work and read the novels of James Baldwin, there was never any mention of either man's sexuality. And even though I still was unaware of my own sexuality, I knew somehow that I was "different." I did not want the same things most of the young women around me wanted, namely a husband and children. I did not know being a lesbian was a possibility. Since I wasn't interested in boys "that way," I simply thought I was not a sexual being.

What saved me was the Beat movement, and specifically the Beat poets: Allen Ginsberg, Peter Orlovsky, Gary Snyder, Anne Waldman, and Ted Berrigan, all of whom became my teachers when I hitchhiked out to Boulder, Colorado, and enrolled in Naropa Institute's Jack Kerouac School of Disembodied Poetics. The Beats were unabashedly sexual. Allen and Peter were clearly a couple; there was also a pair of lesbians on the faculty who made no secret of the fact that they lived together. I learned about Sappho and the island of Lesbos; I learned that Virginia Woolf and Vita Sackville-West were not merely pen pals; I learned that Emily Dickinson had a correspondence with her sister-in-law Susan Huntington Dickinson that some interpreted as romantic. And though these women may or may not have been lesbians, the discovery that women could be primary in each other's lives in a passionate way filled me with a sense of excitement and hope. Finally I realized that I wasn't a freak. There were others like me. A world of possibilities opened up before my eyes.

In 1999, I was invited back to my alma mater to be inducted into the Jericho High School Hall of Fame. The world had changed in many ways since I graduated in 1973. The words "gay" and "lesbian" now appeared in many newspapers across the country on a regular basis, and the gay, lesbian, bisexual, and transgendered community even had its own newspapers and magazines. In 1977, Harvey Milk, the first openly out politician in this country, had been elected as a San Francisco City Supervisor (tragically he was assasinated in his office the following year). Most large cities had gay and lesbian pride parades during the month of June and many high schools had gay straight alliances (Concord High School in Concord, Massachusetts started the first GSA in 1989). The "gayby boom" had begun as more and more lesbians and gay men were starting families, and the gay marriage movement was going strong.

Since graduating from high school, my life had changed dramatically as well. In 1988 I met the woman of my dreams and a year later, on September 10, 1989, we celebrated our relationship with a lifetime commitment ceremony (On September 10, 2004, we renewed our vows before a justice of the peace, making our fifteen-year marriage legal in the state of Massachusetts). I had published close to thirty books, most of which had gay or lesbian content, including the picture book, *Heather Has Two Mommies*, which became one of the most controversial and challenged books of the 1990s. And I had become a political activist, speaking out for the rights of lesbians and gay men every chance I could.

When I was inducted into Jericho High School's Hall of Fame, I was invited to come to campus to give a speech at a school assembly. It was only upon arrival that I was informed that the students knew only one thing about me: I was an author. They did not know the titles of my books and they did not know I was a lesbian. Consequently, I had the unexpected opportunity to come out to an entire high school population. If the students were surprised, they did not show it. Jericho students are nothing if not polite. But they did ask interesting questions. They wanted to know if I had dated boys when I was in high school (yes); they wanted to know how old I was when I came out (twenty-seven); they wanted to know if I wished that I were straight (no, but sometimes I wish my hair was). At one point the questions came to a halt, so I decided to ask my audience, "What is it like for gay and lesbian students today at Jericho High School?" The auditorium was quiet for a moment and then a boy called out, "We don't have any gay students."

About a year later, I received an email from a Jericho High School alumna who graduated in June of 1999. She told me she was a lesbian and had known so since she was fifteen years old. She had been at my induction assembly, but did not feel comfortable coming out in front of her peers that day, or even privately to me. Only after she graduated from high school and went away to college did she feel safe enough to be out. Clearly many things had changed since I'd attended Jericho High School and many things had not.

A book is a powerful thing, and literature can change people's lives. If I had read a biography about a lesbian writer when I was in high school, I truly believe my life would have been vastly different. I might very well have been spared years of pain and confusion because I would have known that a life very much like the one I am now living is possible. If the books in this series had been on the Jericho High School curriculum in 1999, perhaps the young woman who sent me an email would have felt safe enough to come out of the closet before graduation.

It is my hope that this book and others like it will help high school students know that not everyone is heterosexual, and that gay, lesbian, bisexual, and transgendered people can and do live happy, productive, inspiring, and creative lives. The writers included in this series have certainly left their mark on society with their award-winning works of poetry and prose. May they inspire us all to be exactly who we are with pride and celebration.

—Lesléa Newman, 2004

INTRODUCTION

THE GREAT GINZY

Allen Ginsberg was my teacher, my mentor, and my friend. In fact, if it wasn't for "Ginzy" as he called himself, I probably would not have become a writer.

In the early 1970s, when I was a high school student, I was not a happy camper. The limited options that were available to me—heterosexual marriage and motherhood—had all the appeal of jumping into the nearby Long Island Sound with rocks in my pockets. Then somewhere along the way, I read *On the Road* by Jack Kerouac and my life changed forever. I was absolutely ignited by the energy, passion, and rebelliousness of the Beats. In college I devoured other novels written by Kerouac along with the poetry of Allen Ginsberg, Phillip Whalen, Gary Snyder, Anne Waldman, and Diane diPrima. I felt like I understood these writers, and they, undoubtedly would be the only people in the world who could possibly understand me.

So when I heard that the renowned poet Allen Ginsberg was teaching poetry classes at a school he had recently founded along with Anne Waldman, I knew that was the place for me. In 1979, when I was 24 years old, I tucked a well-worn copy of *On the Road* into my back pocket, stuck out my thumb, and hitchhiked across the country, from New York to Colorado to enrolled in Naropa Institute's Jack Kerouac School of

Disembodied Poetics. And not only was I fortunate enough to take classes with Allen, I was picked to be his apprentice.

"Hi, it's Ginzy." he said the first time he called me on the phone. "Come over at two." And so at ten minutes before two, I walked across the then-tiny town of Boulder, Colorado and rang the doorbell of America's most famous (and infamous) poet.

He didn't look much like a controversial poet. Allen, who was 53 at the time, looked more like my Uncle Irving as he shuffled to the front door in his baggy gray pants and rolled up shirtsleeves, his glasses slightly askew, and the top of his bald head shining. Billie Holiday was playing on the stereo, and Peter Orlovsky, Allen's lover of 25 years was standing at the stove in red satin jogging shorts, stirring an enormous pot of soup, his silver ponytail hanging down to his waist, a white dishtowel draped over his arm like a maitre d'.

Allen taught a class called "History of the Beat Generation" in which he expounded on his theories of poetry and the adventures of his friends.

He spoke of rhyme and meter and line breaks, "but," he said, "if you really want to learn how to write poetry, hang out with a poet and watch how his mind works." So that's what I did. My job as Allen's apprentice was to help him answer the pounds of mail that arrived on his doorstep daily. What impressed me was the way he considered every piece of mail of equal worth, whether it was from an important editor, a senator, or a farm boy in Kansas who thought he might be gay and didn't know who else he could confide in. Allen listened while I read each letter aloud and together, we answered them all.

The other part of our time together was spent working on our poetry. Allen thought poetry and the creating of it was a holy undertaking. He took me seriously as a poet, and that attention and care is what allowed me to pursue literature as a lifelong endeavor. All my previous teachers, as well as most of the other adults in my life advised me to get a "real job." My writing "hobby" was nice, but at some point I had to grow up and become practical. Allen thought just the opposite. After all, he had gone through the same struggle as a young man, and had been liberated by a psychotherapist who assured him there was nothing wrong with living his life the way *he* wanted to live it, which was basically exploring relationships and writing poetry. Allen was a living, breathing example of someone who had bucked the system, stayed true to his vision, become of all things a poet, and not only survived, but thrived.

After Allen critiqued my poems, he always brought out a handwritten sheet of paper, read me a draft of a poem he was working on, and asked my opinion of it. He treated me more like a peer than a student, and actually listened to my opinions about his poetry, as if I knew what I was talking about. All I had to go on was my own intuition, which was precisely the point. Allen taught me to get to know and trust my own mind. His often-repeated mantra, "first thought, best thought" is never far from my ear, even now, 25 years later as I sit and write my poems.

After two years, I left Naropa Institute, but I stayed in touch with Allen. I sent him my poems, and he sent back postcards with his feedback: "Solid as a rock, right there, light as a feather." He also wrote "Expose yourself more, both your intelligence and your dumbness."

Allen was the most compassionate, accepting person I ever knew. When he came to my adopted hometown of Northampton, Massachusetts in 1986 to do a reading, I showed up at his sound check. He gave me an enormous hug, and then asked, "So who are you into now, boys or girls?" I told him I had come out as a lesbian and he hugged me again. "I'm so happy for you," he said, giving me a fatherly kiss on the forehead. Since my own father, born the same year as Allen, hadn't had such a joyful response, I greatly appreciated his gesture.

When I heard that Allen Ginsberg had died, I knew it was the end of an era. I also knew I had to bear witness to such a great loss to me personally and to the entire world. Allen's funeral was held at the Shambhala Center in New York City, where he had practiced Buddhist meditation. Hundreds of loved ones, colleagues, friends and students stepped out of their shoes and entered the meditation hall where Allen's memorial service was about to take place.

The service mirrored the richness of Allen's life. First we received meditation instruction and practiced breathing in confusion and fear and breathing out compassion and expansiveness. We listened to Buddhist Monks chant in Tibetan and family members recite Kaddish, the Jewish prayer for the dead. Peter Orlovsky, his silver ponytail long gone, described Allen's last night on earth for us, how he moved "slow as a turtle" to put Ma Rainey on the stereo before he lay down and passed from this world into the next. Anne Waldman and Amiri Baraka read poems.

When the service was over, a spontaneous line formed in front of Allen's coffin, which was draped with a Buddhist flag. I remember marveling at how tiny the casket seemed for a man whose presence loomed so large. One by one, mourners filed sadly by. When my turn came, I knelt down and whispered, "Goodbye, Ginzy" in the vicinity of his ear. And then I found my shoes and stepped out into the streets that Allen would never shuffle down again.

Neil Heims' biography of Allen Ginsberg is a wonderful look at the man behind the legend (for Allen did become a "legend in his own time"). Allen, like all of us, was a flawed human being. He had his obsessions, his neuroses and his imperfections, yet he always tried his best. His loving heart knew no bounds and he was loyal to a fault, even to those who criticized and rebuffed him. He also had a keen eye, a wry sense of humor and a complete commitment to creating poetry. He taught me that inspiration comes from respiration, and that as long as one continues to breathe, one continues to create. As I write these words, I breathe deeply and miss Allen so.

one

Origins

Now to the come of the poem, let me be worthy
& sing holily the natural pathos of the human soul,
naked original skin beneath our dreams
& robes of thought, the perfect self identity
radiant with lusts and intellectual faces

Ginsberg, "Fragment 1956"

PRELUDE: IN THE MIDDLE OF THINGS

On October 13, 1955, in San Francisco, at the corner of Fillmore and Union Streets, in an old garage that had been turned into an art gallery called The Six, Allen Ginsberg threw a rock into the pool of American culture and set off a historical chain reaction of enormous transformative power.

The rock was a poem called "Howl."

AMERICA AT MIDCENTURY

The 1950s in America were characterized by contradictions that the entire machinery of society was mobilized to deny. Despite a few economic recessions, despite a large number of statistically hidden people living in poverty, despite discrimination against blacks, and despite the ongoing Cold War with the Soviet Union and China, there was general economic prosperity and widespread social complacency. Most Americans believed that they had earned the right to enjoy the rewards of having struggled out of the depression of the 1930s, of having defeated Fascism in the 1940s, and of having kept Chinese and Russian expansionism at bay in Korea in the early 1950s. The advent of the television culture and the flood of consumer goods—mercantile and cultural—that television was responsible for marketing fostered a culture in which many people experienced the greatest sense of themselves when they were behaving like conforming members of a homogeneous society.

That there was a threat to American self-satisfaction and a challenge to American comfort was not regarded as a symptom that something was wrong with the American dream and the values upon which it was built, but that outside forces were intent on its destruction. The Communist nations were America's rivals for power in regions strategically or economically important to America. They were dangerous not only because they could launch a nuclear attack against American territory, but also they were insidious because they were depicted as threatening to internally subvert American values, morality, will, and religion. Active inside the United States, communist infiltrators, many believed, could undermine the everyday institutions of America—from the entertainment industry to the labor unions to the schools.

Criticism of any aspect of American life, then, could be interpreted and dismissed as subversive propaganda, as a threat to American national strength and individual morality. An enemy was defined whose very existence demanded the stifling of critical thought, democratic dialogue, dissent, debate, and disagreement—ostensibly to protect them. The battle against Communism, moreover, could be used to justify American military activity and espionage—the coups engineered by the Central Intelligence Agency against democratically elected governments in Iran in 1953 or in Guatemala in 1954, for example. Nonconformist behavior, like homosexuality or Bohemianism, could be vilified and defined as abnormal, ungodly, or un-American; homosexuals or bisexuals, as "security risks." The development, manufacture, and deployment of arms, as well as the atmospheric testing of nuclear weaponry could be justified.

Because nonconformity and dissent were seen as threats to "national security," the conformity and complacency of the Eisenhower years, rather than indicating real social health, were often symptoms of fear and anxiety. People accustomed to challenging and speaking out when they believed in the justice of their argument and in a citizen's right to make an argument now hesitated. They might be seen as subverting the nation's will to stand fast against the "Communist menace" and risked being investigated and punished. The culture of the United States was in large part defined by the "blacklist," which, in fact, put writers, artists, teachers, and intellectuals out of work.

American politics were shaped by ongoing inquiries into people's beliefs and past political activities. The McCarthy committee in the Senate and the Committee on Un-American Activities in the House of Representatives both had the power to subpoena witnesses, compel testimony, and issue contempt citations.

But Newton's third law—for every action there is an equal and opposite reaction—does not operate only in physics. The conformity of the 1950s, the cultural torpor, social complacency, and intellectual passivity, along with conflicted sexuality—the result of the equal influence of puritanism and prurience—produced a huge market for tranquilizers, alcohol, and consumer goods, and fostered the inchoate social reactions of juvenile delinquency and drug addiction. They also established a fertile ground for the growth of a radical Bohemian culture of discontent and an underground of rebellious and visionary artists who, as the defenders of the status quo had long feared, did indeed begin to rise to the surface, to erode the soil upon which American society was grounded, and to challenge the values it held sacred.

When upheaval came, it did not come because of "un-American" foreign agents who hated the principles upon which the nation had been founded or from people with contempt for transcendental values, the sanctity of the individual, or liberty. It came from within American institutions and American traditions. Most visibly, most vocally, and most viscerally, upheaval came from a group of vagabond poets and writers who rebelled against nine-to-five jobs, conventional monogamy, accepted standards of sexual identity, middle-class order, discipline, and taboos: the Beats. It came, in the words of William Carlos Williams, from "the pure products of America." (Williams, 67) Allen Ginsberg, one of the quintessential Beats, was one of the principle voices of that upheaval.

ROOTS

Allen Ginsberg was born on June 3, 1926, in Newark, New Jersey. His mother, Naomi, was born in Nevel, between St. Petersburg and Odessa in Russia. Her father, Mendel Livergant—at Ellis Island his name became Levy—was a businessman, sold Singer sewing machines, spoke Russian as well as Yiddish, wore suits of Western cut, and sympathized politically with the anticzarist revolutionaries. His wife, Judith, bore four children; Naomi was the second. In 1904, Judith and the children moved to Vitebsk and lived with Judith's sister while Mendel and Judith's sister's husband left for America in order to avoid being drafted into the Russian army. After a year, the men had earned enough money to bring their families over to join them. In America, Naomi's parents settled on Orchard Street in Lower Manhattan and opened a candy store. The store prospered. A few years later, they moved from the tenements of the Lower East Side to Newark.

Ginsberg's father, Louis, was born in Newark in 1895. Louis's father, Pinkus, had come to the United States in the 1880s from Pinsk and settled with relatives in Newark. He met Rebecca Schechtman, whose parents came from the Ukraine in the 1870s. They married, opened a laundry, and, with hard work, managed to eke out a living. Ginsberg's parents, Naomi and Louis, met in high school in 1912. They graduated in 1914. Louis went to Rutgers, The State University of New Jersey; Naomi went to a teacher's college. Louis was given a 4F classification during the First World War—because of bad eyesight—and avoided military service.

Like his hero, Eugene Debs, Louis Ginsberg took a pacifist position and opposed the United States's entry into the war. Like Debs, Louis was a socialist. Naomi, a communist, supported America's entry into the war. The differences in their political positions gave rise to arguments, but did not lessen their love. Nor did Louis's parents' objections to Naomi as a daughter-in-law prevent their marriage in 1919. Louis's mother, Buba, was wary of Naomi because of her politics, because she was argumentative, and because early in 1919, after the death of her mother in the influenza epidemic the year before, Naomi suffered a nervous breakdown. The symptoms of the break-down were severe reactions to light and sound. She spent three weeks in bed and then seemed to recover. After their marriage, Louis and Naomi "settled in Newark, near [Louis's] parents. They made an attractive couple: Naomi lithe, energetic and with a good figure; Louis thin, dapper, with small round eye-glasses and his hair brushed back." (Miles, 15)

Louis got a job teaching English at Central High School in Paterson, New Jersey, and taught there for 40 years. Naomi became a special education teacher. The first years of their mar-riage seem to have been happy. In addition to teaching, Louis wrote poetry and was published in newspapers, magazines, and anthologies.

In 1921, Naomi gave birth to Allen's older brother, Eugene, named after Eugene Debs. In 1929, three years after Allen's birth, what might have been a typical depression-era family of left-leaning Jewish Bohemian artists or intellectuals was destabi-lized and profoundly redefined by the renewed onset of Naomi's mental illness which proved to be severe, recurring, and lifelong.

NAOMI

In 1929, Naomi survived a difficult operation for pancreatitis, but was left with garish abdominal scars. Worse, the trauma led to her second mental breakdown. Her life became a succession of mad, sometimes violent, episodes and of long hospitaliza-tions. She was given strong medication and electroshock treatments. She suffered from paranoia and persecution mania, from depression and dementia. She was plagued by delusions. She believed Louis's mother was trying to poison her, that Buba was the head of a spy network out to get her, that Louis had given his mother money he had actually used to pay for Naomi's sanatorium care, that there were hidden microphones in the ceiling, that President Roosevelt had placed wires in her head in order to gain access to her private thoughts, that wooden sticks had been driven into her back, and that her son Allen was not her son. She berated Louis, railed at him, and taunted him with an affair she claimed to have had with the Bohemian poet Maxwell Bodenheim when they were first married and attended poetry meetings in Greenwich Village. (Caveney, 22; Miles, 24–25) She wandered naked through the streets near their home. Once she locked herself in the bathroom and slit her wrists.

In 1929, when Naomi was admitted to the Bloomingdale Sanatorium near Tarrytown, New York—Allen was three years old—Louis and the children lived in:

> a run-down Jewish neighborhood of shabby apartment buildings, wood-frame houses, warehouses, small workshops, and produce markets. Bridge Street, a block away, led down to the Passaic River, where the warehouses and factories gave way to slums, and black people lived in old frame houses.... The Erie Railroad crossed the street, and beyond the tracks was a huge red-brick factory that produced silk thread, one of Paterson's major industries. Its constant rattle was heard in the Ginsberg apartment. Spools of defective silk and empty cardboard cones littered the area. (Miles, 17)

Ginsberg's childhood was defined by a mad, unstable mother, whom he loved and whose love he craved, and a strong, loving, and rock-steady father, who worked hard to keep things

together. It was under those conditions that Ginsberg's character was shaped. Since she was often able to function in
routine matters, Allen could hardly know when something
Naomi said was mad and when it was not. Even when she was
not ill, Naomi—being a communist and a nudist—practiced
ways of thinking and of living which were often at odds with
mainstream society. When he was around 14, Naomi insisted
that Louis was plotting against her and that he, Allen, had to
help her escape from the house and check into a rest home. He
reported later:

> I was a prisoner in the house. I was smaller than she was and
> she was intimidating me to do this. She was splitting my
> mind because I didn't know if she was right or not. She said
> she was being persecuted and it didn't make sense but she
> was so insistent about it. (Miles 31–32)

Allen's life was continuously disrupted by his mother's illness,
whether she was at home or in a hospital. When he visited her,

> [i]t stank, sour smell of wards, disinfectant, vomit, piss,
> people incontinent. And I remember walking down the
> wards, there were all these old people lined up, crooning to
> themselves, singing, talking to themselves, snapping their
> fingers, shadow boxing, usually in sloppy ill-fitting clothes.
> Some of them had been left there for years by their families.
> (Miles, 22)

One of the ways he coped was by writing about what was going
on. Although the horrors of his life affected him, by chronicling
them he also kept them at a distance. By writing, everything—
what happened in the world around him and what happened as
responses inside him—could be treated as if it were "part of"

the "external phenomenal world." (Ginsberg, *Cosmopolitan Greetings*: xiii) It is one of the marks of his poetry that Ginsberg could make a panoramic scan of the surface of all his awareness, seamlessly shifting from the perception to what he perceived with the steady gaze encompassed by his long-breath lines.

By the age of 11, Ginsberg was keeping a journal, a practice he continued throughout his life, producing hundreds of volumes of introspective and reflective prose and verse. On June 19, 1937, for example, he wrote, "My mother thinks she is going to die and is not so good." The next day, "My mother is worse." The next, "I stayed home to mind my mother." Two days later, "My mother locked herself in the bathroom early in the morning and my father had to break the glass to get in. She also went back to the sanatorium." Mixed with these matter-of-fact observations of highly charged emotional events are other, more ordinary, comments: "I got a haircut and two pair of shoes and heard the 'Louis-Braddock' fight over the radio. Louis won and is now champion of the world." (Miles, 25) After he broke the glass panel of the bathroom door, Louis found Naomi naked and with bleeding wrists. He bandaged them and put her to bed. "The boys stood there, shivering in their night clothes, panic in their eyes." In the morning an ambulance came for Naomi. (Miles, 25)

Despite the calmness of his journals, Naomi's madness was obviously deeply troubling. At the end of his life, Ginsberg spoke of his feelings of division, guilt, and rejection:

> My father rejected me if I didn't believe him, and if I didn't believe her stories, she would reject me. So in order to win *her* affection, I would have to believe her delusions. It's a double bind that leaves a permanent sense of guilt. (Miles, 527)

He was also confused:

> I was putting on a stiff upper lip and trying to fulfill the obligations I thought were demanded of me, taking over my father's role of taking care of my mother ... and having to be the recipient of her confessions and emotions but of a delusional nature. And that confused me, I didn't think I was confused but really I had a kind of split mind, of who I was supposed to trust. (Miles, 37)

Perhaps, also, of *how* he was supposed to be: intuitive, but irrational, like his mother or firm and "rational" like his father? Both aspects entered his psyche, formed his character, and defined its conflicts. And both also represented strategies for winning love.

The traumatic experience of a having a mother with mental illness seems to have served as a sort of inoculation for Ginsberg, allowing him, later, to go to the heart of, to stand in the center of, perilous, threatening situations and survive. Having a rationally coping, calm father to balance his wild and erratic mother seems to have imposed in him a similar balancing force that insured a rational consciousness even within apparently irrational situations. Throughout his adulthood, repeatedly, Ginsberg found himself or placed himself at the center of dangerous, frightening, and irrational situations—his early habit of taunting established authority, the derangement of Beat experience, the terror of terrifying drug trips, the danger of political confrontations, the violence or madness of people he esteemed and loved. Yet he was able to stay calm and useful at the center of the tempest and focus his awareness, often by means of retreating into or calling forth poetry and, later, Buddhist chanting.

The first day of kindergarten—Naomi was in Bloomingdale

sanatorium—Allen was so troubled that he yelled and screamed until Louis came for him. After Naomi returned from the sanatorium, Allen, playing with matches, accidentally set fire to a rattan wastebasket she had made for occupational therapy, and was unable to stamp out the flames. The apartment filled with smoke. Louis was summoned home from school and fire engines were rushed to the house. Throughout his childhood, Ginsberg was subject to awesome experiences of loneliness and infinity: "my heart would ache and I would go into some kind of swoon thinking how mysterious the universe was and how lonely I was in it." (Miles, 29) He had fantasies of sadomasochistic anal eroticism and genital exhibition, and experienced crushes on other boys—with shame. Sometimes he slept in the same bed with his father and experienced states of sexual arousal, and sometimes he slept with his brother, but when he tried to snuggle with him, Eugene just pushed him away. "I must have been a sexpest to the whole family, even when sleeping with Louis. Gene was the only one who rebuked me, but without shame or guilt, just elastic rejection of elastic demand," (Miles, 26) Ginsberg reported years later. Most significantly, he could not get real mother love from Naomi.

The intervals when his mother was sane and when his father could be relatively carefree were also significant in the formation of Ginsberg's personality and his interests. Ginsberg recalled Sundays at home when he would read *The New York Times* and his father would walk around the apartment reciting Milton, Shelley, or Dickinson. They spent summers, when his mother was well, at a Communist Party Jewish camp, Nicht-Gedeiget (No-Worry) in upstate New York. There were political arguments between his parents over the Moscow purge trials and the Soviet invasion of Finland. In this kind of environment, Allen developed a keen sense of political awareness and commitment.

He assembled a large file of clippings from *The New York Times* about world events—a practice he continued throughout his life, documenting things like U.S. government involvement in illicit drug trafficking. He also supported the intervention of the United States in Spain on the side of the Loyalists against Franco and was passionate in his opposition to Hitler and Mussolini. In high school, Ginsberg was head of the debating club and argued against isolationism. He worked in the congressional campaign of a local C.I.O. union organizer, and wrote letters in support of him to the local newspaper when his opponent branded him a "Red." He was in the theater club in high school and enjoyed performing as a ballerina in a ballet burlesque, surreptitiously flirting with the football players, who were also in drag for the show. And he wrote essays for the school magazine. He was popular, and described himself as a kid with

> [big] eyeglasses and a thin face with buck teeth, going to an orthodontist to have them fixed. A kind of mental ghoul, totally disconnected from any reality, existing in a world of newspapers and aesthetics: Beethoven, Leadbelly, Ma Rainey, and Bessie Smith. (Miles, 29)

In his high school yearbook, he was described as "the philosopher and genius of the class." Probably the most profound experience in high school happened when, one afternoon, his English teacher

> read aloud verses from Walt Whitman's "Song of Myself" in so enthusiastic and joyous a voice, so confident and lifted with laughter, that I immediately understood "I wear my hat indoors as well as out ... I find fat no sweeter than that which sticks to my own bones" forever. (Miles, 30)

He had crushes on several boys in high school, too, one a gymnast, another— with whom he "was totally in love"—was "my high school mind hero, jewish [*sic*] boy who became a doctor later." Allen "spent all the time I could with him, but in a very shy way." The boy was a year ahead of him in school and during Allen's last term was already studying at Columbia University. Half because of his enchantment with this boy, Allen decided to go there, too. Standing on the Hoboken ferry on his way to take the entrance exam for Columbia, he promised himself—perhaps in part as the sublimation of what seemed like an impossible love—that he would devote himself to the working class and become a labor lawyer. (Miles, 35)

chapter
two

Influences

Naïve, he was incredibly naïve! He was just an eager young Jewish kid from Paterson who wanted to know everything about books and writers and art and painting.
—Lucian Carr

AT COLUMBIA

Allen Ginsberg won a scholarship to Columbia and chose prelaw as his field of study. But a variety of influences drew him away from law, though not away from his resolution to work against injustice and exploitation. First there were his teachers in the Columbia English Department. The poet and critic Mark Van Doren, literary editor of *The Nation* magazine and a friend of Robert Frost, had won the Pulitzer Prize for Poetry in 1940. Raymond Weaver, a Melville scholar, wrote the first biography of Herman Melville, *Mariner and Mystic*, and discovered the manuscript of *Billy Budd* in a trunk in the attic of a house on Twenty-Third Street. Ginsberg was awed by him: "The man who discovered posthumous manuscripts of Melville. That's *really* a professor!" (Miles, 38) Lionel Trilling was a well-known literary critic. In his classes he "raised questions about how we live our lives, about the nature of good and evil, about the roles played by culture and biology, about our ambivalence in making moral choices." (Glick, 86) While his staid temperament and cautious conclusions visibly diverged from those that have come to define the radically defiant Bohemianism of Allen Ginsberg, the root impulse of his concern—searching for "the best kind of truth"—did not. Elegant and reserved in demeanor, Trilling was the first Jew to be a professor in the Columbia English Department. The first semester at Columbia, Ginsberg immersed himself in the great writers of Western Civilization, explored the city, went to museums, and went—with Naomi—to the opera.

The students in the English Department also formed an impressive group. Ginsberg became friendly with John Hollander, the poet and scholar. In a review years later in the *Partisan Review*, Hollander wrote that he did not like "Howl," but included a number of Ginsberg's poems in his later anthology of contemporary poetry, *Poems of Our Moment*.

Ginsberg did not become friendly with Norman Podhoretz, another classmate. Podhoretz became the editor of *Commentary* magazine, a neoconservative luminary, and a lifelong antagonist. Lucien Carr, however, was the classmate that had the greatest influence on him and, indeed, played a pivotal role in defining the poet and the person Allen Ginsberg became. Carr introduced Ginsberg to William Burroughs, Jack Kerouac, and Arthur Rimbaud.

Burroughs and Kerouac were contemporaries, friends, and literary colleagues. Just as Ginsberg changed the course of American culture with "Howl," so did Kerouac with *On the Road*, which became a kind of Boy Scout Manual for the Beat Generation; and William Burroughs, exploiting the vision bestowed on him by morphine addiction and crime, wrote *Naked Lunch*. Arthur Rimbaud, the French Symbolist poet, died in 1891. Rimbaud's outlaw life—his cruel love affair with the poet Paul Verlaine, whom he tormented so fiercely that Verlaine tried to shoot him, his renunciation of poetry before he was 20 to become a gunrunner in Africa, his early death, and his poetics of synesthesia (the process of describing one sensory experience in terms of another)—made him a Beat icon, precursor, and role model. Ginsberg's explanation of Rimbaud's poetics sounds remarkably like Ginsberg's own:

The poet becomes a *seer* through a long, immense, and reasoned *derangement of all the senses*. All shapes of love, suffering, madness. He searches himself, he exhausts all poisons in himself, to keep only the quintessences. Ineffable torture where he needs all his faith, all his superhuman strength, where he becomes among all men the great patient, the great criminal, the great accursed one—and the supreme Scholar! For he reaches the *unknown!* (Miles, 43)

Ginsberg met Lucien Carr in December 1943 during his freshman year and was immediately taken with him. Carr was "the most angelic-looking kid I ever saw," he recalled. (Miles, 37) Carr lived in the same dorm as Ginsberg, and as Ginsberg was going to his own room one evening he heard the Brahms Clarinet Quintet. He knocked on the door of the room from which it was coming and Carr opened it. On the walls there were reproductions of paintings by Henri Rousseau and Paul Cezanne. Among the books were Spinoza's *Ethics*, Hardy's *Jude the Obscure*, and Rimbaud's *A Season in Hell* in the French. Carr and Ginsberg sat up all night drinking wine and talking about literature, art, and how to live. Carr invited Ginsberg to go to Greenwich Village with him Saturday night to meet some friends. Ginsberg wrote excitedly to his brother, "Saturday I plan to go down to Greenwich Village with a friend of mine who claims to be an 'intellectual' ... and knows queer and interesting people there. I plan to get drunk Saturday evening, if I can. I'll tell you the issue." (Miles, 39) Ginsberg felt a giddy world of thought and experience opening to him.

The first time Carr took Ginsberg down to the Village, they stopped at the apartment of David Kammerer. Kammerer was older than Carr, had been his Scoutmaster back in St. Louis, had developed an intense, morbid—because unreciprocated—erotic fascination with Carr, and had followed him from one prep school to another and then to Columbia. Although Carr disdained Kammerer and rebuffed his sexual advances, he kept him hanging on and teased him. Sometimes he allowed him to trail along when he took a girl out for a drink. In the present instance, Carr was introducing a new friend to Kammerer. Certainly, he gave Kammerer mixed signals, and despite his abjurations, Carr's girlfriend, Celine Young, was convinced, "Carr felt ... pride in having Dave dog his footsteps." (Miles, 53)

That first Saturday night, Kammerer was asleep, so Carr took Ginsberg to the Minetta Tavern and the two got drunk, but they went back to the Village a few days later and stopped at the apartment of William Burroughs. Kammerer had known Burroughs in St. Louis and introduced Carr to him when Burroughs came to New York. Burroughs, 30, was 13 years older than Ginsberg. He had been drafted during the war, but was quickly released with a psychological discharge when the Army learned he had cut off the last joint of his little finger a few years earlier to impress a boyfriend. When Ginsberg and Kerouac were arguing once about what *is* art and if art needed an audience in order to exist, Burroughs settled the matter, saying, "That's the stupidest question I ever heard of," and explained that it depended how "you want to define the word 'art'" because "[w]ords don't have a built-in definition. If you want to define this as art, then you define it as art. If you don't want to use that word for that situation, then you don't. But to argue whether the thing is art or not is obviously a confusion in terms." Ginsberg was delighted "to hear such iconoclastic sense." (Miles, 47) Burroughs's library was a treasure of authors Ginsberg had not yet come upon. At their first meeting, Burroughs gave Ginsberg a copy of the poetry of Hart Crane, the alienated poet of "The Bridge," who struggled with his homosexuality, revealed himself mainly through the complex imagery of his poetry, and drowned himself. Burroughs also introduced Ginsberg to William Blake, the late 18th century visionary English poet who became a living presence for Ginsberg.

Through his teachers at Columbia, Allen Ginsberg entered a world of academic intellectuals for whom literature, whether in its study or practice, was what Matthew Arnold prescribed culture ought to be, a pursuit of sweetness and light. Carr introduced Ginsberg to a world of underground, Bohemian, sometimes criminal, intellectuals and writers for whom the use of literature was essentially the aggressive assertion of their alienation from the constraints of their culture. He also challenged Ginsberg's political idealism. The two argued about the conflict between Carr's stance of elite decadence and Ginsberg's devotion to the class struggle. "'You want to be a labor lawyer?' Carr asked when they were standing outside a tough working class bar. 'You've never worked a single day in your life!'" (Miles, 43)

At the West End Bar, a popular student hangout near the university—the drinking age in New York was 18 at the time—Carr met a Barnard girl named Edie Parker. She shared a room with a journalism student named Joan Vollmer. Sometimes Carr and his girlfriend would use Edie's place to make love

Being Queer

Poet, novelist, and social critic Paul Goodman was one of the members of the New York avant-garde underground in the 1950s who met at the San Remo Bar on the corner of Bleecker and MacDougal Streets. In an essay on the experience of homosexuality before Gay Liberation, Goodman wrote:

> In essential ways, my homosexual needs have made me a nigger.... [I]t is not taken for granted that my out-going impulse is my right.... I don't complain that my passes are not accepted; nobody has a claim to be loved (except small children). But I am degraded for making passes at all, for being myself.... [T]here is a way of rejecting some one that accords him his right to exist and is the next best thing to accepting him.... Allen Ginsberg and I once pointed out to Stokely Carmichael [Black Power activist] how we were niggers, but he blandly put us down by saying that we could always conceal our disposition and pass. That is, he accorded us the same lack of imagination that one accords to niggers; we did not really exist for him. (Stoehr, 216)

or to spend the night. It was there that Carr met Jack Kerouc. Kerouac had been at Columbia on a football scholarship, had become interested in literature, antagonized his coach, and flunked out. He joined the navy, didn't fit in, and got discharged by acting crazy, and then became a merchant seaman. Carr and Kerouac immediately became friends. They got drunk together and had long conversations about art and literature or played goofy pranks. One night, for example, Carr rolled Kerouac up Broadway in a barrel. Towards the end of the war, ostensibly for Carr to get away from Kammerer, they set sail on a freighter to France so they could be there for the expected liberation. They got as far as Albany, New York. This sort of aimless quest for kicks came to define the Beats. Carr was sure Ginsberg and Kerouac would hit it off and gave Ginsberg Kerouac's address. And they did, particularly because Ginsberg saw the Kerouac who lived beneath the hipster façade.

In *Vanity of Duloz,* Kerouac described their first meeting in May 1944:

> I was sitting in Edie's apartment one day when the door opens and in walks this spindly Jewish kid with horn-rimmed glasses and tremendous ears sticking out, seventeen years old, burning black eyes, a strangely deep voice. (Miles, 44)

Ginsberg's recollection of their meeting was of "being awed by him because I'd never met a big jock who was sensitive and intelligent about poetry." Kerouac was "shrewd," "gruff," "inquisitive," "compassionate," "with a golden heart," and Ginsberg saw himself as an "awkward kid." (Miles, 45) He fell in love with Kerouac immediately, and it was a love that never left him despite Kerouac's later insults, betrayals, hostility, and rejection.

What brought Ginsberg and Kerouac together—apart from Allen's sexual attraction to him—was a shared sense of a spiritual mystery hidden behind their material experiences. They both intuited that there was something unreal or ghostly about the real world. They had both sensed the immensity of the universe and the sad isolation of each person from others. And they both had experienced intimations of the unity of all being. In Ginsberg's words, they believed, "Everyone has the same soul. We're all here together at one and the same place, temporarily, with a totally poignant tearful awareness that we're here together." (Miles, 46)

SEXUAL DESIRES AND THEIR VICISSITUDES

At Columbia Ginsberg was the same person as the kid in Paterson who had longed for love. He was gratified to find himself with so many friends. In a letter to Eugene, Ginsberg wrote, "I am happy to say that, unlike Paterson, I have accumulated a modest number of close friends, some neurotic, some insane, some political. To categorize, I have three circles of acquaintances: first the madmen and artists from Greenwich Village and Columbia," whom he named and described: Carr, Kammerer, Kerouac—"one of the most interesting"—among others. In the second circle were "sensitive youths" and "young intellectuals," classmates who were making translations of Sir Thomas More's *Utopia* and writing conventional sonnets. In the third were people he had daily commerce with, like several of his roommates. (Miles, 56) There are two characteristic things about Ginsberg in this letter—1) his practice, which becomes a formal, organizing aspect in much of his poetry, of cataloguing: counting, listing, and categorizing things; and 2) his clarity of perception. Committed to his friends, nevertheless, he had no illusions about them and could make distinctions: "some neurotic, some insane, some political." From the first group

Ginsberg derived his identity and with it he formed his own future and the future—it is not exaggerating to say this—of American culture, style, values, and consciousness.

The group around Carr formed a league dedicated to overcoming the values of conventional society, which they considered hypocritical and rigid. They were determined to live free, honest, open lives, guided by an awareness of "the idea of transience of phenomena. Everybody lost in a dream world of their own making. That was the basis of the Beat Generation," Ginsberg recalled in an interview in 1986. (Miles, 65) The means by which they chose to assert this new consciousness, the "New Vision," was literature. The artist, when truly an artist, they believed, following Rimbaud, was a seer. To be artists in this way required living without restraints. "Art," in Ginsberg's words, "is merely and ultimately self-expressive." Therefore, "we conclude that the fullest art, the most individual, uninfluenced, unrepressed, uninhibited expression of art is true expression and the true art." (Miles, 47)

The sense of this group as a heroic, even if partially nuts, band of rebellious brothers sharing a new social vision—both communal and individualist—more valid and more humane than the vision governing the established order was seriously shaken for Ginsberg when Lucien Carr stabbed David Kammerer to death in Riverside Park. Around midnight on the night of the murder in August, 1944, Kammerer confronted Carr at the West End distraught that Carr had been avoiding him. When the bar closed they took a bottle and went to the park and continued drinking and arguing. Kammerer apparently made sexual advances. Perhaps he was violent. Carr stabbed him twice in the heart and threw the body into the Hudson. Afterwards, Carr went to Burroughs's apartment, told him what happened and that he expected he'd "get the hot scat." They shared a "last cigarette," and Burroughs gave him five dollars, told him not to "be absurd," to tell his family, get a good lawyer, and turn himself into the police. Next Carr went to Kerouac. With Kerouac as lookout, Carr threw the knife down a sewer and buried Kammerer's glasses in Morningside Park. They went to Times Square, ate hot dogs, saw a movie, and went to the Museum of Modern Art. Then Carr went to his psychiatrist's office and finally to an aunt's apartment and contacted the family lawyer.

When Carr turned himself in, the police did not believe him and refused to book him. The next day Kammerer's body was found floating in the Hudson. Charged with murder, Carr was sent to the Tombs in lower Manhattan. Burroughs and Kerouac were arrested as material witnesses. Burroughs's father bailed him out; Kerouac's father told him to "go to hell!" When Kerouac asked his girlfriend, Edie Parker, for help, her family's lawyers stipulated only under the condition that they get married. They did while he was in jail. Carr was sentenced on a charge of second-degree manslaughter to Elmira Reformatory in upstate New York and was released after 18 months. After his release, he got a job as a reporter for United Press and continued to work for that organization, advancing to senior positions, until his retirement. He remained friends with Ginsberg, Burroughs, and Kerouac, but generally withdrew from public association with them. When Ginsberg published "Howl" in 1956, Carr's was one of the names on the dedication page of the first edition; Carr asked Ginsberg to remove it, which he did, although it remains in the text of the poem itself.

Ginsberg was not involved in Kammerer's murder. He was, however, significantly affected by it. Ginsberg was homosexual, uncomfortable with it, and had not revealed himself to his friends. Carr's defense at his trial was that Kammerer was homosexual and that he (Carr) was not. He had, therefore, killed Kammerer to protect himself from a perverse sexual advance. That the court was convinced that Carr was not homosexual and the victim of homosexual solicitation and of possible rape turned what could have been a first-degree murder charge into second-degree manslaughter with its relatively light sentence. Beside this inevitably disturbing aspect of the defense for Ginsberg—exploiting the stigma attached to homosexuality—the murder showed that the Bohemianism that Ginsberg had begun to value had a troubling and dangerous side. But the dark aspect of the human character and the violent behavior of people close and dear to him was not a new experience. Just as he had dealt with his mother's breakdowns by writing about them, so the young Ginsberg attempted to deal with the breakdown in his community.

For a creative writing class at Columbia during the fall semester, Ginsberg began a novel using the Carr-Kammerer story as its basis. After he showed the first chapter to his teacher, however, he received a letter from one of the assistant deans of Columbia asking him not to write about the subject. In person, Dean Nicholas McKnight told Ginsberg that the university did not want any more negative publicity, that his book was "smutty" and that Kerouac was a "lout." Until this encounter, Ginsberg had not felt alienated from the culture of the university. His Bohemian and his academic development had been complementary. Now he was shocked and disillusioned by Columbia's attempt to censor his writing. Now, too, the dean became concerned about Ginsberg and began keeping an eye on him. McKnight received reports from the bartender at the West End that Kerouac and Ginsberg were often there drinking till closing time. McKnight called Ginsberg and his father to his office and reprimanded Allen, threatening to take away his scholarship, despite the fact that he was making straight A's. As a result of this meeting, Ginsberg moved into Livingston Hall on the Columbia campus. But he did not stop seeing Kerouac.

Ginsberg and Kerouac continued their conversations about a "New Vision," and about changing cultural consciousness through their writing. Ginsberg also continued to see Burroughs and was greatly under his influence. Fueled by conversations with Burroughs, Allen argued with his father that "an immoralist can confirm 'enduring human values.'" His father wrote back "You're all 'wet' Allen. You simply have little experience in life ... Your sophistry ... is a series of half-truths, verbal cleverness, and dangerous ideas expressed in specious and dextrous verbiage." Burroughs, Louis wrote, was "dangerous, not because he rationalizes but because his end product of thought and attitude results, eventually, if carried out in action, in danger and disharmony and chaos." Louis ended his letter to Allen with a challenge: "Where is your former zeal for a liberal, progressive, democratic society?" Then under his signature, (with an anxious memory of Naomi?) he added the question, "What about a psychiatrist?" (Schumacher, ed., *Family Business* 6–7) Ginsberg's career as a poet and as a public figure shows that he took his father's admonition seriously. In all his work there is an attempt to explore the forces of the unconscious through candor and creativity and to neutralize the brutality he believed repression created. In this way he hoped to realize social justice and assert the inviolability of individual humanity.

Shortly after Lucien Carr's arrest, during a series of intense conversations and soul-searching, Ginsberg told Kerouac, "I'm really in love with Lucien. And I'm really in love with you. And I really want to sleep with you." In a 1972 interview Ginsberg explained, "I knew [Kerouac] was going to accept my soul with all its throbbings and sweetness and worries and dark woes and sorrows and heartaches and joys and glees and mad understandings of morality, 'cause that was the thing he had." (Miles, 55) Kerouac's response, according to Ginsberg, was a groan, "He suddenly saw this great chasm of moral perplexity opening up in front of him for the rest of our lives … His groan wasn't rejection. It was a groan of dismay. But he didn't want to make it with me." (Miles, 56)

For about half a year more they did not "make it" together. Their friendship deepened because they shared the desire to be great writers and to change American culture, to make it more open, candid, and spontaneous than it was, more receptive to personal vision and personal expression, less codified regarding what was acceptable behavior. In their estrangement from society, they needed each other for a sense of community. Kerouac was tormented by life and art. He spent the days writing and burned what he wrote each evening. He repeatedly walked out on Edie Parker and then called her back to him. Burroughs, more than ten years older than Ginsberg and Kerouac, had taken on the role of teacher and analyst. He disturbed Kerouac one evening telling him his difficulties stemmed from an unhealthy attachment to his mother, that Kerouac was holding his mother's apron string and walking around her in a wide circle, but that as time went on, the string would get shorter and the circle would get smaller. (He was right.) Afterwards, Kerouac visited Ginsberg in his dorm room in Livingston Hall on the Columbia campus. They spoke about what Burroughs had said, and Kerouac slept over in Ginsberg's room, not as a lover; they were like any pair of friends. Ginsberg's roommate, Bill Lancaster, later told the dean.

At 8:00 the next morning, the Assistant Dean of Student-Faculty Relationships burst into their room and evicted Allen. He was fined two dollars and thirty-five cents for "entertaining an unauthorized guest overnight," informed that "the privilege of residence at Livingston had been withdrawn" because he had given "overnight housing to a person who was not a member of the college and whose presence on the campus was unwelcome," and was suspended from Columbia. He was also reprimanded for "obscene writings on his window." The cleaning woman routinely neglected to clean the windows of his room and Ginsberg had traced two incendiary slogans on them: one a denigration of the sexual potency of Nicholas Murray Butler, then president of Columbia, and the other a strong obscenity combined ironically with a slur against Jews— ironic because Ginsberg was reacting to the disrespect and contempt he felt directed against him by the cleaning woman and the university. The anti-Semitic obscenity did not reflect his sentiments. The cleaning woman reported the graffiti to Columbia's Dean Furman, who had also been Keroauc's foot-ball coach.

Mark Van Doren came to Ginsberg's defense, to no avail. In an interview Dean McKnight insisted "Mr. Ginsberg, I hope you realize the *enormity* of what you've done." Ginsberg acted contrite and said, "Oh, I do, sir! I do! I do! If you can only tell me what I can do to make up for this." McKnight told him he would not be able to return to Columbia until he had worked at a job for a year, seen a psychiatrist regularly, and could pro-vide a letter from the psychiatrist attesting to his maturity and responsibility. In a 1974 interview, Ginsberg lamented:

> So I was kicked out of Columbia, but the thing that rang in my ears was "Mister Ginsberg, I hope you realize the *enor-mity* of what you've done!" because I actually hadn't done anything. I wanted to. I lay there longing all night. (Miles, 59–61)

ON THE STREET

Suspended from Columbia and barred from living on campus, Ginsberg moved into the large apartment that Joan Vollmer, Edie Parker's former roommate, had rented on New York's

Upper West Side. Edie and Kerouac were staying in the apartment, as was a Columbia student named Hal Chase. Ginsberg took a series of odd jobs: welder at the Brooklyn Navy Yard, dishwasher, clerk at the Gotham Book Mart, coat checker in a nightclub. With William Burroughs he began exploring the criminal scene around Times Square.

Burroghs and Ginsberg went to the bars and met hoodlums, thieves, prostitutes, and drug users. Burroughs became a "fence," receiving and unloading stolen goods. When Burroughs had several boxes of Syrettes, single-dose morphine syringes, to get rid of, a small-time hood he knew introduced him to Herbert Huncke, a thief, male hustler, and junky, who bought the morphine. Huncke also showed Burroughs how to shoot up. After that, Burroughs joined Huncke and his cohort Phil White rolling drunks in the subway, collecting material for his novel, *Junky*. Ginsberg did not participate, but he got to know Huncke. Through Huncke and White, Benzedrine was introduced into Joan Vollmer's apartment, and everyone, including Ginsberg, began using it.

Ginsberg also began openly exploring the homosexual world. He went to a bar on MacDougal Street in the Village and was picked up by an older sailor, but found the experience cold and distasteful. At the Museum of Modern Art a few weeks after that, Ginsberg met a student his own age and went home with him. "I wasn't much taken with him emotionally," Ginsberg later told an interviewer. "It was just a relief to have somebody physical." (Miles, 66) About six months after the night Kerouac had slept in Allen's room in the Columbia dorm, Ginsberg and Kerouac did "make it." It was under the old, elevated West Side Highway in lower Manhattan, by the trucks, an area famous for male cruising and sexual encounters. Kerouac was disturbed by his occasional forays into homosexuality. "It automatically repels me," he wrote Ginsberg after a sexual evening spent with

Burroughs and some other men, "causing me a great deal of remorse and disgust." (Miles, 68) Nevertheless, he did allow himself occasional sexual contacts with Ginsberg. Ginsberg was always grateful to him:

> He was bending and stretching quite a bit to accommodate my emotions. That's why I've always loved him, because I was able to completely unburden myself and express my deepest feelings and he could relate to them. Reject them, hear them out, reciprocate sometimes[;] actually go to bed with me sometimes, rarely. Get drunk with me, walk around, being there, hearing me through and giving me a reaction to bounce off against. So I was more intimate with him about my feelings than with anybody on earth. I bared myself to him and he was able to take it. (Miles, 68)

In August 1945, Ginsberg joined the United States Maritime Service—the Merchant Marines—to make some fast money. He graduated from the training school in November and was released to active duty. His time in the service was uneventful. He scrubbed floors, washed dishes, and read Hart Crane's poetry. He did not have trouble following the rules and enjoyed time off at Manhattan Beach. But he contracted pneumonia and spent much of his time in sick bay writing letters and reading novels. When he graduated, Ginsberg was a member of the Seamen's Union. Immediately he shipped out as a messman on a freighter to Norfolk, Virginia. Then he got a job on a coal barge that unloaded at New Orleans. On this voyage he first smoked marijuana.

Nineteen forty-six, Kerouac wrote, "was a year of evil decadence." Ginsberg returned to Joan Vollmer's apartment. Kerouac and Edie were often there. Burroughs moved in after Kerouac and Ginsberg introduced him to Joan and they became lovers. Huncke was often around, and he brought Alfred Kinsey over when Dr. Kinsey came to New York to gather data for what would become a landmark study of American sexual behavior. Kinsey had contacted Huncke because as a hustler in Times Square he had a good knowledge of the underground sex scene. Kinsey interviewed Vollmer, Kerouac, Burroughs, and Ginsberg. Everyone at the apartment, including Ginsberg, was getting high and exploring "deviant" and even criminal behavior. Burroughs was using morphine; Ginsberg and Kerouac, Benzedrine and amphetamines. What Kerouac saw as a year of evil decadence, however, Ginsberg saw as a period of profound radical exploration of consciousness. Of his drug use Ginsberg later explained:

> The whole point of smoking grass or taking peyote was as a probe, an examination of what is the alteration of consciousness caused by amphetamine, or morphine, or marijuana or heroine, or peyote, or mescaline. At least that was my terminology then. Examination, like William James's experiments with nitrous oxide very much in mind. (Miles, 73)

Ginsberg and Burroughs explored hypnotism and telepathy, Burroughs psychoanalyzed Ginsberg and brought him to tears with the realization that he felt that "Nobody loves me!" Ginsberg later said, there "was a kind of breakthrough for me, a realization of my actual feelings. Painful feelings I didn't want to admit at that age, nineteen." In a letter he wrote at the time, Ginsberg told Burroughs that his analysis has "illustrated what I have dimly known, I feel more guilty and inferior by reason of faggishness than intellectualizations will admit is proper." (Miles, 72) He had come to realize that he felt that having homosexual desires made him shamefully inferior. This was a widespread, socially inculcated, socially approved feeling at the time. It had its foundation in mainstream attitudes of the sort Ginsberg's father expressed in a letter to him in 1945. Speaking theoretically, not about his son (at least, not consciously)—Allen had not come out to him—in an ongoing argument (resulting from Allen's admiration for Burroughs) he was having with Allen about "normal" and "abnormal values," Louis Ginsberg wrote, "… you would bracket the rationalizations of a homosexual or an insane person as satisfactory for society and for the person. The homosexual and the insane person is [sic] a menace to himself and to society. Danger and disaster lie that way." (Schumacher, ed., *Family Business* 6) It seemed natural and reasonable to him to place homosexuality and insanity in the same category. The psychiatric profession did.

Kerouac sketched a picture of Ginsberg in 1946 in *The Town and the City* that remained true throughout his life. Kerouac described Ginsberg as:

> an eager, intense, sharply intelligent boy of Russian-Jewish parentage who rushed around New York in a perpetual sweat of emotional activity, back and forth in the streets from friend to friend, room to room, apartment to apartment. He "knew everyone" and "knew everything," was always bearing tidings and messages from "the others," full of catastrophe. He brimmed and flooded over day and night with a thousand different thoughts and conversations and small horrors, delights, perplexities, deities, discoveries, ecstasies, fears. He stared gog-eyed at the world and was full of musings, lip-pursings, subway broodings—all of which rushed forth in torrents of complex conversation whenever he confronted someone. (Miles, 74)

The overwhelming impression is of Ginsberg's immense energy and the extent of his contact with people. Twenty-two years later, in a Profile in *The New Yorker*, Jane Kramer described the same qualities:

> One of Ginsberg's friends has called him the central casting office of the underground. He enters in the address book that he always carries in his purple bag the name, address, and phone number of anyone he meets who plays, or is apt to play, a part in what he thinks of as the new order, or has information that might be useful to it, and he goes to considerable trouble to put people he likes in touch with each other and with sympathetic and influential Establishment characters who might be helpful to them. In this way, he has managed to create a network of the like-minded around the world. Any one of his friends who goes to a city that Ginsberg has ever visited knows in advance where to stay, whom to see, and what local statutes to avoid breaking, not to mention who the local shamans are, what politicians are friendly, who has bail money, who sells pot, the newspapers, the phone numbers of the local activists, and where the best sex and the best conversation can he found. (Kramer, "Paterfamilias—I" 36)

At the same time that Ginsberg was exploring the caverns of the underground world and of his own submerged self in 1946, he was reading not just decadent and rebel authors like Rimbaud, Hart Crane, and Louis-Ferdinand Celine, but Henry James. He was working on the novel that unnerved the deans of Columbia University and writing poetry. He was seeing his mother and visiting his aunt and uncle in the Bronx. Throughout his life, even as he traveled to the far edges of Bohemia, Ginsberg remained connected to his family.

He had an ongoing correspondence with his father, which continued until Louis's death in 1976. Much of it has been published in a volume of over 400 pages. There was a deep love and an easy candor between the two even as they argued fiercely about poetry and politics. Ginsberg held within himself both his mother's experience of "the skull beneath the skin," and his father's buoyancy, capability, and sense of responsibility. Louis stayed with him through experiences that would have caused a rift between many parents and children. Louis encouraged Allen to keep his common sense, to remember the Greek ideal of moderation, to appreciate the value of self-discipline, (Schumacher, ed., *Family Business* 8) to "walk balanced between the seen world and the unseen one." (Miles, 75)

In his own way, Ginsberg did, although it might not have appeared so. By September of 1946, the scene at Joan Vollmer's apartment had become toxic and dangerous. Burroughs was addicted to morphine and Vollmer was having psychotic episodes because of her use of Benzedrine. Benzedrine use was causing Kerouac to lose his hair, and his skin became so grey that he sometimes wore make-up when he went out. Ginsberg smoked pot and hopped himself up with Benzedrine and amphetamines. But in the middle of the chaos and disintegration, he sat at his typewriter working on a long poem, "Death in Violence." (In the spring of 1947, that poem won the first prize of $110 in the biannual George Edward Woodberry Contest at Columbia.) And although he was on suspension from Columbia, he remained in contact with Lionel Trilling, Mark Van Doren, and Raymond Weaver, kept his post as an assistant editor of the *Columbia Review*, the student literary magazine, and published poetry and reviews in all its 1946 issues.

Herbert Huncke and Phil White were using the apartment at 115th Street to hide stolen goods and to store weapons. Burroughs was writing fake prescriptions for himself and when he misspelled "Dilaudid" (a form of morphine), the pharmacist called the police. Burroughs was arrested. His father bailed him out. Burroughs was given a four-month suspended sentence and went back to St. Louis with his father. Huncke and White moved into the apartment. Then Huncke was arrested and sent to the Bronx County Jail for drug possession. White moved out, and Vollmer cracked up and was sent to Bellevue. Ginsberg left the apartment, too, and went to stay with his father in Paterson until the end of September. When the fall semester at Columbia started he moved back into the city to a room on West Ninety-Second Street.

NEAL CASSADY

Ginsberg was readmitted to Columbia in September 1946. Dean McKnight required that he present a psychiatrist's letter. Ginsberg wrote it himself, and got a doctor who had been one of his mother's psychiatrists to sign. "He takes good care of his personal appearance," it read, "and shows adequate attention to the various necessary amenities of social intercourse. In my opinion, there is no question, that at the present time he is psychologically pretty much as sound as they come." But he wasn't. The intellectual excitement of his first year of Columbia had given way to a sense that the school honored a moribund and reactionary spirit, that there was little place for the vision he was pursuing. In 1968, he told Jane Kramer,

> You can't imagine what colleges were like in those days. The whole system of shutdown and provincialism extended to the academy.... at Columbia, Whitman was hardly taught.... John Crowe Ransome and Allen Tate were like the supreme literary touchstones. Joyce and Lawrence were the property of funny modernist[s] ... considered eccentric by the rest of the faculty. My course in the American novel went up to Edith Warton [sic].... No Gertrude Stein.... it would have been scandalous to put Henry Miller in the curriculum, not

because he was dirty but because he wasn't even thought of as a writer. [William Carlos] Williams was an unknown factor…. In economics, they had like Louis Hacker teaching the triumph of capitalism. In history, it was Jacques Barzun, who was just teaching politeness. Anthropology was more or less dead. And the French Department was filled by old, sour-tempered professors whose idea of contemporary French literature was a few reactionary novels written about 1910…. I was actually going to Burroughs for all my reading lists. (Kramer, "Paterfamilias—II" 72)

Emotionally, Ginsberg was pained by loneliness and longing. "Things going ill; poetry stopped, reading desultory, neurasthenic sleeping, loneliness, splenetic moods, boredom, fear, vanity," he wrote in his journal on November 25. He was wracked by unsatisfied homosexual desire and by torment at even feeling such desire. But he also experienced periods of high energy and euphoria, often the result of using pentaphon, an opium derivative, Benzedrine, and marijuana. (Miles, 80–81)

In January 1947, Ginsberg met Neal Cassady. Handsome, energetic, charming, seductive, sexually athletic, fickle, promiscuous, a car thief, and a con artist, Neal Cassady has become a Beat Generation legend. Friends and lovers adored him. The energy of his charm overcame the faults in his character. When Ginsberg met him, he was married to a girl named LuAnne. She was 17. Like Ginsberg, he was 20. Having spent his youth hanging around pool halls with a drunken father and in reformatories, he was streetwise. By the age of 21, Cassady had stolen, by his account, over 500 cars. He was the model for Dean Moriarity, the central character of Kerouac's *On the Road*, and for Cody in Kerouac's *Visions of Cody*. Kerouac credited Cassady with being the one who showed him how to write by the spontaneous speech-like prose of his letters. In the early

1960s Cassady joined Ken Kesey (author of *One Flew Over the Cuckoo's Nest*) and his group of acid-dropping vagabond hippies, the Merry Pranksters. He drove their fabled Day-Glo bus and became a literary character again—in Tom Wolf's *The Electric Kool-Aid Acid Test*.

When Ginsberg met Cassady, they connected immediately. "Two keen minds they are, they took to each other at the drop of a hat," Kerouac wrote, in *On the Road*. "Two piercing eyes glancing into two piercing eyes ... Their energies met head on." The night they met, Kerouac and Ginsberg walked Cassady up to the place in Harlem where Cassady was staying with the cousin of a friend of Kerouac. Because it was too late for Kerouac to travel back to his parents' house in Queens, Cassady suggested he and Ginsberg stay the night and they could all have breakfast in the morning. Kerouac slept in a double bed with the cousin, and Ginsberg and Cassady shared the other bed. When they got into bed, "Allen lay with his back to Neal, balancing on the edge of the narrow bed, careful to keep his distance. But Neal stretched out his arm and pulled Ginsberg to him, murmuring, 'Draw near me.'" (Miles, 82–83) For Cassady it was a simple thing to do, even if what followed would be far from simple. Cassady was impulsive, tried everything, and lived in the moment. He liked thrills, took risks, and he was good at intuiting other people's needs and gratifying them when it gave him a charge. Ginsberg was needy, not impulsive. He was candid about his desires, but in a sad, begging confessional way. So when Cassady embraced him, what to Cassady was the pleasure offered by the present moment, to Ginsberg was a dream of fulfillment to which he surrendered with all his heart:

> I lay with my hair intermixed with his, he asking me 'What shall we do now?'

—And confessed, years later, he thinking I was not queer
at first to please me & serve me ... or if I were queer, that's
what I'd likely want....

But I made my first mistake, and made him then and
there my master, and bowed my head, and ... showed him I
needed him ... for my dreams of insatiety & lone love. (Ginsberg, *Collected Poems, 1947–1980*, "Many Loves" 156)

They spent the next two nights together "staring into each
other's eyes, finding out whether we bugged each other and
what the limits were." Their affair was tempestuous. Ginsberg's
journal, January 21, 1947: "Having spent a wild weekend in
sexual drama with Cassady, I am left washed up on the shore of
my 'despair' again. It is after such like pleasure that I get full
knowledge of what I have closed myself off from." Throughout
February, Ginsberg's head was full of the variety of sexual experiences the two of them shared and he wrote down all the
possibilities in his notebook. He transformed the physical into
a spiritual excitement, defining sex with Cassady as "a sort of
joyful yoga." He wrote that Cassady "transformed it into a spiritual social thing as well as a matter of esthetic prowess." Sex
between them was "an ultimate exchange of soul." (Miles, 84)

The relationship was, like Ginsberg and Cassady themselves,
unstable. On March 2, Ginsberg wrote in his journal, "I think
he does no longer excite me. I've almost used him up in a way
[and] loved him as much as I can, to no end, except final loss of
real feeling and love, and want no more of him." Ginsberg
explained later, that it seemed to him then that the relationship
"wasn't reciprocal." Cassady went back to Denver. Ginsberg had
planned to visit him there once the spring semester at
Columbia was over, but was not sure he would until he received
a letter: "I need you now more than ever," Cassady wrote. Every
day I miss you more and more.... Let us ... find true awareness

by realizing that each of us is depending on the other for fulfillment." Soon after, however, Cassady wrote,

> I *really don't* know how much I can be satisfied to love you, I
> mean bodily.... I, somehow, dislike ... men & before you,
> had consciously forced myself to be homosexual, now, I'm
> not sure whether with you I was not just forcing myself
> unconsciously.... You meant so much to me, I now feel I
> was forcing a desire for you bodily as a compensation to you
> for all you were giving me. (Miles, 85–86)

When Ginsberg arrived in Denver, Cassady was divorcing his
wife, LuAnne—although he still slept with her—and had fallen
in love with Carolyn Robinson, a Bennington graduate, with
whom he was living.

Ginsberg rented a room in Denver. When his money ran
out, he moved in with Neal and Carolyn and slept on the floor.
This created an impossible situation. He soon found a job at a
department store as part of the evening cleaning crew, and
rented a cheap basement room. Neal was seeing the three of his
lovers and several others on a kind of round-robin schedule,
but, as he had warned Ginsberg, he had lost sexual interest in
him. He stood him up many nights. The more he withdrew, the
needier Ginsberg became. He spent dismal and lonely nights
waiting.

> I have been developing ... hallucinations about the tele-
> phone. The vacuum cleaner has a high singing pitch and I
> began last night, awaiting Neal's call, to confuse it with the
> dull ringing of the telephone. It reached such a point
> tonight, combined with an emotional exhaustion and an
> intellectual despair, that I was completely paralysed for min-
> utes on end, stop-ping work turning off the motor, listening,

half-hearing the phone. I had a vivid auditory sensation several times, that in the confusion, it really was the phone, and dropped my work, and ran over to the phone, and found it dead and silent. At one point I could not continue work and collapsed in a chair. (Miles, 87–88)

As usual, no matter what the situation, he kept writing poetry and doing sketches in prose.

Towards the end of the summer, the dynamics of Ginsberg's relationship with Cassady changed again. Ginsberg was planning to go to Texas, where Burroughs and Joan Vollmer, now married, lived. Burroughs was growing marijuana. Herbert Huncke was managing the business. Burroughs was still addicted to morphine; Joan, to Benzedrine. She was pregnant. William S. Burroughs III was born addicted to morphine, alcohol, and Benzedrine. Ginsberg convinced Cassady to go with him. Cassady told Carolyn that he was going to try to be homosexual for Allen's sake. Carolyn told him he might do as he liked but that she was going to San Francisco to live with a friend and slept elsewhere. When she came by in the morning to say goodbye she found Cassady in bed with both LuAnne and Ginsberg.

Ginsberg and Cassady hitchhiked to Burroughs's farm. Ginsberg, still hung up on Cassady, was trying to forge a deep bond with him and overcome the sense of loveless loneliness that ate away at him. It is hard to say what Cassady wanted or thought he was doing. For a while, however, he was going along with Ginsberg's wishes. In Oklahoma, they "kneeled together on the road ... in the middle of a four way cross of dirt roads, on an endless plain at night fall," and vowed "fidelity, union, seraphic insight." Ginsberg hoped by this ritual "to accomplish a transfer of heart, and vow to stick with each other" and be lovers spiritually, if not physically. (Miles, 90)

By the time they got to Burroughs's farm Ginsberg had become intolerable to Cassady, not just sexually. Cassady wrote to Kerouac that he "couldn't stand Allen to even touch me … he was all opening up and I was all …" He left it at that. Ginsberg for his part was going through the romantic agony of realizing that "the sacramental honeymoon is over…. he [Cassady] means what he says when he says he can't make use of me sexually," but "wondering what will happen to Neal if I really withdraw my active queer love and leave him alone emotionally." (Miles, 91–92) It was useless speculation. Cassady insisted they split up and Ginsberg went the next day to the National Maritime Union Hall and signed on to a coal ship going to Dakar, French West Africa. The trip meant taking a leave of absence from Columbia for the fall semester. He was gone for a total of 50 days. He wrote, "The Monster of Dakar," and smoked a lot of marijuana.

During all the turmoil with Cassady, Ginsberg stayed in touch with his father by letter. He reassured him, when he shipped out to Dakar that "I have never understood your angle in your fear that somehow … I will leave college uncompleted. That is the furthest thing from my mind, to go into the world sans the B.A., even, in fact, an M.A., so don't worry about me becoming a permanent wastrel." (Schumacher, ed. *Family Business* 16) Ginsberg wrote his father, furthermore, "I am aware of your … anxieties about me, and have anxieties about myself equal and much greater, so you must trust me to work things out. That is all that would be done, anyway, whatever happens." (17) He intended, he explained, just because of his own anxieties, to go into analysis, and hinted at his homosexuality saying "if you knew (Horrors, alas, too terrible to indite!) my sexual & soul-ful difficulties you would bless my efforts." (15)

chapter
three

Catastrophe

There I was, in the dark, in an apartment in the middle of Harlem, whirling like a dervish and invoking powers. And everybody I tried to talk to about it thought I was crazy.

—Allen Ginsberg

BACK IN NEW YORK CITY: A VISION

In November 1947, Ginsberg returned to New York City to a frantic, Dostoyevskian life characterized by madness, crime, transforming visions, and spiritual redemption. The doctors at Pilgrim State Hospital were pressuring him to authorize a prefrontal lobotomy for Naomi; his impossible longing for Neal Cassady kept him in a state of continuous sexual and emotional frenzy; he was cruising promiscuously, drinking heavily, taking Benzedrine and morphine, and staying up all night. Even so, he was working at a part-time job, writing poetry, and working on a novel. He wrote to Wilhelm Reich, whose character-analytic vegetotherapy combined Freudian psychoanalysis with a systematic attack on neurotic defenses through techniques of breathing and muscular manipulation, hoping to find a therapist:

> I have been a homosexual for as long as I can remember, and have had a limited number of homosexual affairs, both temporary and protracted. They have been unsatisfactory to me, and I have always approached love affairs with a self-contradictory, conscious masochism.... I have had long periods of depression, guilt feelings.

He also told Reich of his analysis with Burroughs, which had made his situation worse: "The inevitable and unfortunate effect was that it left me washed up on the shores of my neurosis with a number of my defenses broken, but, centrally unchanged, with nothing to replace the lost armor." (Miles, 96)

Ginsberg began going to Allan Cott, one of the practitioners Reich's assistant had recommended. Since Cott's office was in New Jersey, Ginsberg could visit his father after his sessions. He told him of his homosexuality. Louis was troubled by the revelation and by a fear that Allen might be "seriously disturbed," like his mother. Burroughs's reaction was just the opposite of Louis Ginsberg's. Louis agreed with a core tenet of the Reichian understanding, that without the establishment of a heterosexual libidinal economy there is no psychic health. Burroughs, on the other hand, objected to the Reichian doctrine of heterosexuality. (Miles, 96) The therapy, in any event, had powerful effects on Ginsberg, which he later compared to some of his experiences with the drug *ayahuasca (yage)*. But the therapy did not last long enough to accomplish anything. Cott told Ginsberg that smoking marijuana might lead to a "psychotic episode," and terminated his treatment because Ginsberg would not stop.

About his drug use, particularly about smoking marijuana, Ginsberg wrote later in life, "Our original use was for aesthetic study, aesthetic perception, deepening it." (Miles, 97) It was part of the project to derange the senses, in the manner Rimbaud had decreed, in order to achieve a profound contact with primal experience at its unconscious level, before it is organized by the guides that culture gives for organizing and controlling experience and perception. The Beat exploration of consciousness was an attempt to excavate the unconscious and, by bringing it to the surface, make fundamental alterations in conscious awareness and the pursuit of being human. Within aesthetic boundaries, what might have been an unnerving psychotic experience could become an inspiring visionary/poetic experience. Sometimes, it might be difficult to tell them apart or to keep one from becoming the other. For Ginsberg, the line between madness and creativity, between psychosis and inspiration, was thin—indeed, never so much as during this period, which would end with his incarceration in the Long Island House of Detention and his subsequent commitment to the Columbia Presbyterian Psychiatric Institute.

Ginsberg used pot to help him, he maintained, explore the aesthetics and the dynamics of the unconscious. After examining

Cézanne's watercolors at the Museum of Modern Art, for example, Ginsberg wrote, "I got a strange shuddering impression looking at his canvasses, partly the effect when someone pulls a Venetian blind, reverses the Venetian—there's a sudden shift, a flashing that you see in Cézanne canvases." (Miles, 97) He referred to this phenomenon—which he called "eyeball kicks"—later in "Howl" as making "incarnate gaps in Time & Space through images juxtaposed," as "trap[ping] the archangel of the soul between 2 visual images," as "join[ing] the elemental verbs and set[ting] the noun and dash of consciousness together jumping with sensation...." (Ginsberg, *Collected Poems, 1947–1980*, "Howl" 130)

During the spring term in 1948, Ginsberg was living on 114th Street and seeing Kerouac, who was finishing *The Town and the City*. He kept in touch with his father and Edith, Louis's friend and Ginsberg's future step mother, and even took Kerouac to the Passover Seder at their house. But he also once asked Kerouac to hit him, he felt so bereft of any feeling of contact. With Mark Van Doren's encouragement and under his guidance he assembled a book of poems, *The Denver Doldrums*, but his spirit was as oppressed as ever. In April he heard from Neal Cassady, who told him that he had married Carolyn and that she was pregnant. Ginsberg sent back ironic and bitter congratulations; Cassady parried with a note saying Ginsberg was "way, way, way off base. You and I are farther apart than ever. Only with effort can I recall you." (Miles, 98) Ginsberg's work at Columbia suffered considerably, too. By the end of the term, he owed Trilling a paper, he was doing badly in math and organic chemistry, and he had neglected to register for the required gym classes. At the end of May he sublet an apartment in Harlem, worked as a file clerk, and took morning classes at Columbia, spent a good deal of time walking through Harlem or staying in his apartment, alone, spinning sexual fantasies and reading mystical Christian texts.

One hot summer day, stretched out in bed by the open window, shuttling between sexual reverie and looking through the poetry of William Blake, Ginsberg came upon "Ah Sunflower," a poem so long familiar to him that

> it didn't make any particular meaning except some sweet thing about flowers—and suddenly I realized the poem was talking about *me* ... and suddenly ... I heard a very deep earthen voice in the room, which I immediately assumed, I didn't think twice, was Blake's voice.... [T]he auditory hallucination ... the apparitional voice in the room, woke me further deep in my understanding of the poem, because the voice was so completely tender and beautifully ... ancient.... I suddenly realized that *this* experience was *it!* ... that this was the moment that I was born for. (Caveny, 53–54) My body suddenly felt *light* ... it was a sudden awakening into a totally deeper real universe than I'd been existing in.... I was sitting in the middle of an entire planetary solar system! ... I had the impression of the entire universe as poetry filled with light and intelligence and communication and signals. Kind of like the top of my head coming off, letting in the rest of the universe connected to my own brain. (Miles, 100)

All the transcendental longing of the poem burst upon him and the conflict between the limitations of the terrestrial world and the infinite openness of a diaphanous infinity, unbounded, was resolved in the breath of the voice he heard reading to him. The voice, wonderfully enough—although Ginsberg did not make the connection then—is a description of his own voice, as anyone who has heard it can attest: "a very deep earthen voice." Kerouac had called it "a strangely deep voice." Years later, Ginsberg did think of the voice as a voice "of his own mature self." (Ball, ed., *Journals* xiv) It was a mystical hallucinatory experience in which Blake the creator bestowed his largess upon Ginsberg, conferring upon him his voice, the voice of the poet/seer who bridges the worlds of time and eternity by existing in both.

The experience of a transcendental consciousness was so powerful to Ginsberg and so absolute in its revelation of the human essence that it created a longing in him to reside within it as his ongoing way and it altered the way he saw others. Soon after this experience, for example, he was in the Columbia bookstore. Looking at the clerk, he thought:

> *he* knew also, just like I knew.... everybody in the bookstore knew, and ... they were all hiding it! They all had the consciousness, it was like a great unconscious that was running between all of us, that everybody was completely conscious, but that the fixed expressions people have, the habitual expressions, the manners, the mode of talk, are all masks hiding this consciousness. Because almost at that moment it seemed that it would be too terrible if we communicated to each other on a level of total consciousness and awareness each of the other.
>
> The complete death awareness that everybody has continuously with them all the time [was] all of a sudden revealed to me at once[:] the faces of the people ... *hiding* the knowledge from each other. Having a habitual conduct and forms to prescribe, forms to fulfill[, r]oles to play. But the main insight I had at that time was that everybody knew. (Miles, 102)

Louis Ginsberg was frightened by Allen's vision. It seemed too much like Naomi's insanity. After Allen told him about his experience of Blake's presence and the accompanying sense that he had seen God—Louis was an atheist—they argued about the existence of God. When Allen showed him his poetry, Louis wrote:

> It's got some weighty thought … but I can't say that I'm sure of what you mean. Your piece seems knotty…. The main idea, even if I mutilate it in simplification, is that your real self is struggling to be free from the false selves or neurotic influences which cling to and hamper it. What I like about your piece is the play of lambent wit about it … and the "sound effects." (Schumacher, ed., *Family Business* 20)

He encouraged Allen to do his schoolwork, not to be anxious about the future, and to "work steadily and regularly at your last paper for [Jacques] Barzun." Regarding Cassady, he advised, "Put a tourniquet around your affection." (*Family Business* 24) That was not so easy to do: Cassady had begun writing friendly and sexually flirtatious letters again.

At Columbia, when Ginsberg spoke of his vision of Blake, Lionel Trilling and Allen's other teachers, except for Mark Van Doren, thought he had finally gone crazy. The best proof that he had not—the work he would produce, a direct outcome of this state of mind—was yet to come.

Through all this turmoil, Ginsberg was working as a copy boy at the Associated Radio Press News Service in Rockefeller Center, going to school, reading, writing, listening to music, smoking pot, visiting friends, and spending a great deal of time with Kerouac and other incipient Beat writers like John Clellon Holmes. In December, Neal Cassady returned to New York with his first wife LuAnne, having left Carolyn and their new baby (but he would return to her shortly). Herbert Huncke was also around again and moved into Ginsberg's Harlem apartment. In a 1969 newspaper column, Louis described the scene:

Louis Ginsberg, Poet

Allen Ginsberg's father, Louis, was a poet who was published widely in newspapers, magazines, and several anthologies. He was a member of the New Jersey Chaucer Guild and the Manuscript Society. In 1937, he borrowed $2000 to pay for the publication of a collection of his poetry, *The Everlasting Minute*. (Miles, 27) His poems are traditional, well-made lyrics in the manner of A.E. Houseman. Here's a poem of his called "April":

Even when all my body sleeps,
  I shall remember yet
The wistfulness that April keeps,
  When boughs at dusk are wet.

The haunted twilight on the lane;
  The far-off cricket's croon;
And beautiful and washed by rain,
  The mellow rounded moon!

So, underneath the waving grass,
  And underneath the dew,
April, whenever you will pass,
  My dust will dream of you!
  (*http://www.bartleby.com/273/24.html*)

This is a poem Louis wrote in 1959 called "To Allen Ginsberg":

Almost like Theseus, you grope
Through dank, subterranean passageways
Of your different selves.
Through neon nights and dead-end days,
You fumble at and explore
Many a bewildering corridor.
You are your own labyrinthine maze.
May you soon see
The Ariadne-thread
Of your true identity
To find the sun-burst opening ahead.

                              (Hyde, 84)

[F]ate dredged up from the side of humanity a person called Hunkie [sic], a junkie. Early in Allen's life, when Allen was living in [Harlem], I came to visit him and noticed that a new overcoat I had bought him was missing. A typewriter was gone, too. "Where are they, Allen?" He confessed that Hunkie had stolen them and pawned them for money for a fix.

On my next visit, who was there, lying on the couch, but Hunkie. When he saw me, he sidled out.

"Allen, what's this?" I asked. "How can you let him in when he robbed you?

Allen spread his hands apart and replied, "What else could he do? He was desperate."

Later, Allen sublet an apartment of a literary friend who had an elegant library and fine records. It was not long before Allen noticed that books were missing. Who else was taking them but Hunckie?

He's helpless, he's struggling for survival," said Allen.

I remonstrated, criticizing Allen for his irresponsible attitude toward someone else's property.

I'll pay back the amount ...," he said.

To make a long story short, we bought books at a Fifth Avenue store to make up the loss. Allen's father paid the bill. (Schumacher, ed., *Family Business* 284–285)

Soon after he moved into Ginsberg's Harlem apartment, however, Huncke was sent to Rikers Island for marijuana possession. When Ginsberg's friend Walter Adams left for France, Ginsberg took over his three-room apartment on York Avenue ($14.95 a month).

When Huncke got out of jail, it was winter and he wandered around New York City for three weeks, homeless. Finally, he showed up famished with bleeding feet at Ginsberg's door and

Ginsberg took him in, cared for him, and restored him to health and strength. Huncke, using his helplessness and neediness, quickly took over most of Allen's apartment, including his bed. Worst, it would turn out, he was using the apartment as a depository for stolen goods. On Easter Sunday, 1949, Ginsberg got a letter from Burroughs telling him that he had been arrested for narcotics possession and that the police had seized his papers, which included letters from Ginsberg talking about the possibility of selling the pot Burroughs was growing in New York. Burroughs warned that Ginsberg's apartment might be searched. Huncke and his associates assured Ginsberg that even if the police did come they would not notice the stolen goods, but Ginsberg insisted they get the hot stuff out.

They loaded a car with it in order to move it to another location and Ginsberg asked to be dropped off at his brother's place, where he would leave some of his journals and Burroughs's incriminating letters. "Little Jack" Melody, one of Huncke's associates and the driver of the car, took a wrong turn up a one way street. A policeman signaled him to stop; he pedaled the accelerator and fled. There was a chase, blaring sirens, shots fired. Making a sharp turn, "Little Jack" hit a curb and a lamppost; the car turned over, Ginsberg got out unhurt, returned to his apartment, and within an hour was arrested. The police had found his address among the papers scattered near the car. The caper made all the papers, including the front page of the *Daily News* where Ginsberg was portrayed as "a boy-wonder … a brilliant student genius … plotting out big criminal scenes … addicted to drugs and this gang kept me supplied and forced me to mastermind robberies." (Kramer, "Paterfamilias—II" 81) Later, Ginsberg wrote that at the time "for some desperate reason of vanity or fear, I was manoeuvering myself, and everyone I knew, into some immediate catastrophe." (Miles, 114) The catastrophe—in tandem with his hallucinatory encounter with Blake the year before—heralded the end of his apprenticeship as a poet. It gave him "Howl" and he became a world-renowned figure.

AT THE COLUMBIA PRESBYTERIAN PSYCHIATRIC INSTITUTE

At Columbia, Ginsberg's arrest was one more blow to the prestige of the university. Nonplussed by Ginsberg's behavior, Lionel Trilling nevertheless took him to see Herbert Wechsler, a professor at the Columbia Law School. Wechsler advised Ginsberg to plead insanity and commit himself voluntarily to a mental hospital and then plead guilty at his trial. Trilling gave him the name of a psychiatrist, Dr. Fagin. After seeing Ginsberg, Dr. Fagin testified that Ginsberg was seriously disturbed and needed hospitalization. Ginsberg apparently was at his wit's end. He wrote to Kerouac:

> I have manoeuvred myself to a position I have always fancied the most proper and true.... I really believe, or want to believe, really I am nuts, otherwise I'll never be sane.... I've gotten so hung up on myself now it isn't funny anymore. I stop in the middle of conversations, laughing shrilly—stare at people with perfect sobriety and remorse, and then go on cackling away. (Miles, 119)

Ginsberg told Jane Kramer, "I was thinking all the time: What am I doing? What am I going through, having visions and ending up in jail? What *is* reality? Is it my vision or Huncke's void, or what's actually going on?"

Ginsberg was trying to understand himself and his values in relation to Huncke, who seemed to him to embody a criminal saint. But he was not sure. Perhaps Huncke was just a person with a cruel streak who caused others pain? In a conversation with Van Doren, Ginsberg asked if he really had to *choose* between criminals and society. Van Doren told him he did, that if he "believe[d] that Huncke was some sort of criminal saint or illuminated being, then" he had "to follow through with your choice and perhaps even go to jail for your beliefs." (Miles, 119) When Allan Cott, Van Doren, and Lionel and Diana Trilling all attended the trial and testified on his behalf, Ginsberg wrote to Kerouac, "I feel grateful … That's what Van Doren means by society I suppose, people getting together to keep each other out of trouble (or away from tragedy)." (Miles, 120)

Ginsberg also wondered about his "own cruelty, making everybody unhappy." He felt guilty that when Louis was burdened with the expense of caring for Naomi, who was then out of the hospital and living in New York City, he had become an additional expense. His legal fees came to one thousand dollars, which his father and his brother Gene paid. But he nevertheless felt a conflict regarding the source of his identity. He felt estranged from his father and brother and wanted to identify with his mother. One night at Naomi's sister Eleanor's,

> I suddenly became angry at Eleanor, and inwardly sickly at my brother because they patronized and baffled and fogged the natural exuberance and innocent perception of Naomi; however, Naomi too started compulsively blindly questioning me in repeated monotones, about my travels, which she's half forgotten, till I became weary of all…. I feel I could half start a conspiracy of the insane with her, underground— but she goes blank and mechanical often. (Miles, 120)

Until there was a hospital bed available, Ginsberg stayed with Louis and Edith in Paterson. On June 29, 1949, the evening before he was admitted to the Columbia Presbyterian Psychiatric Institute, Ginsberg wrote in his journal:

I have been wrathful all my life, angry against my father and all others. My wrath must end. All my images now are of heaven. I dream of incomprehensible love and belief. I think always that I am about to put an end to my life, only now there is no worry as to how I will do it, as last summer after the vision. In the hospital I hope to be cured. My images tell me that the hours of truth are at hand. I am not going to die, I am going to live anew. (Miles, 121)

A few days later, he was less ebullient, but still clear in his introspection:

[W]hat a terrible future[!] I am 23, the year of the iron birthday, the gate of darkness. I am ill. I have become spiritually or practically impotent in my madness this last month. I suddenly realized that my head is severed from my body, I realized it a few nights ago. (Miles, 121)

Beside this mind body split, which he would confront repeatedly throughout his life, Ginsberg faced a conflict between the values of his father and teachers at Columbia and those advanced by Burroughs—his Falstaff, absent the girth, and his renegade father and teacher. At this stage of his development, it was Burroughs's ways Ginsberg rejected. "I have discovered that I have no feelings, just thoughts, borrowed thoughts," Ginsberg wrote Kerouac regarding Burroughs's influence. Writing to Kerouac after Allen's arrest, Burroughs postured,

If I was in Al's place I would say, "Go ahead and place your charges, if any." His present position is insufferable. Imagine being herded around by a lot of old women like Louis Ginsberg and Van Doren. Besides I don't see why Van Doren puts in his 2 cents worth. Sniveling old liberal fruit." (Miles, 122)

Ginsberg's response when Kerouac reported this was generous. He did not remind him how Burroughs had escaped his own arrests through his father's intervention, nor did he blame Burroughs for his baleful influence. Putting himself inside Burroughs head, instead, he imagined the web of tensions conflicting attitudes can provoke. He wrote Kerouac,

> O Bleak Bill, he is afraid that I will find out that he is crazy, that his analysis of me was a tragic farce—not an absurd farce, but a tragic real one—that he has led me astray. Reality, as [Bill] well knows, is that familial and social community which we, as madmen, have discontinued. (Miles, 122)

The stay at the hospital was not grim. He was not subject to electroshock treatments or given psychotropic medication. Ginsberg spoke with psychiatrists a few times a week. The goal was adjustment, conformity to the norms of heterosexual society. He realized quickly that he must keep quiet about his vision of Blake, his feelings, his desires, and the world he envisioned. "I think," Ginsberg said later, "if I had argued a lot I could have got myself into a lot of trouble." He recalled,

> In our first week's conversation, I was trying to explain to him where I was at, and I said, "It's like the telephone is alive." Now, had he been a doctor of any kind of wit … he would have said, "And what does the telephone say, Allen?" But instead he got annoyed and stamped his foot and said, "The telephone is *not* alive." So he didn't know where I was at all. (Kramer, "Paterfamilias—II" 54–55)

Ginsberg was allowed to leave the hospital daily from 4:00 to 7:00 P.M., and on weekends from 4:00 P.M. on Friday until Sunday evening as long as he was accounted for, and he was able, therefore, to spend time with Kerouac and Cassady, who was back in New York, having left his wife—who was pregnant with their second child—and having taken up with a young woman whom he had also gotten pregnant.

Ginsberg wrote Burroughs that he still wanted to work in the labor movement. Burroughs vituperated in a letter to Kerouac, "I fear the U.S. is heading for Socialism.... Allen ... has been utterly corrupted by those liberal psychiatrists. He talks of becoming a labor leader! I wrote him what I think of labor leaders, unions and liberals.... Allen is aligning himself with a cancerous element that will stifle every vestige of free life in the U.S." Ginsberg responded,

> Really, dearie, we know so little about home economics that all this b.s. about Stateism ... and welfare state is just a W.C. Fields act. Vow for my part, it would make things no worse for me if we had socialism. Trouble with you is you never had to work for a living. As for me, I have nothing better to do than to help those less fortunate than myself. (Miles, 123)

But Ginsberg was not destined to do that as a labor lawyer. "I was sitting in the reception room" at the Columbia Presbyterian Psychiatric Institute, he recalled in 1968:

> with my valises, waiting to be shown a bed.... when all of a sudden this guy Carl Solomon ... comes up out of the depths of the hospital from a shock streak and waddles over to me. He's in this giant bathrobe looking very fat—because of I think insulin and metrasol. And he looks at me and says, Who are *you*? So I say, "I'm Myshkin." "I'm Kirilov," he says. (Kramer, "Paterfamilias—II" 83) [Myshkin is the saintly hero of Dostoevsky's *The Idiot*, Kirilov, the nihilist in Dostoevsky's *The Possessed*.]

Carl Solomon was a suicidal genius, nihilist, and avant-garde rebel. Following a notion Andre Gide put forth in the novel, *Lafcadio's Adventures,* he had been committed for performing a "gratuitous act: stealing a peanut butter sandwich and then reporting himself to the police and requesting a lobotomy." He had spent time in Paris, joined the Communist Party, lived with a prostitute, seen Antonin Artaud—the mad genius revolutionary who invented the "theater of cruelty"—perform. (Miles, 118) At the hospital, he introduced Ginsberg to Artaud's ideas and to Jean Genet, the great homosexual French novelist and poet, who had spent much of his life as a thief and a drag queen until he was imprisoned in France and finally released from a life sentence because of a petition from Jean-Paul Sartre and a number of other leading French intellectuals. Solomon made Ginsberg see that the poet not only must connect with the sensitivity of the human spirit but with its brutality. And it was Solomon's awareness of the symbiosis of a mad psyche and a disordered society that was at the root of Ginsberg's culture-busting poem "Howl."

Beginning Again

*Today my family should all dance under
the blooming cherry tree in the back
yard.*

—Allen Ginsberg

AT HOME

After seven months, Ginsberg left Columbia Presbyterian to live with Louis and Edith in Paterson. Edith later told him that in private a psychiatrist from the Institute had warned them that Allen was "partly homosexual," that "if you really want to have a close relation, you have to accept that, even to the point of receiving his lovers in your home, and if you want a really close relation, of allowing them to stay over." Ginsberg later said, it "did a world of good because my father believed in authority, and if that was the word, it relieved him of the necessity to come down hard and worry and be scandalized." But there was little need for Louis to worry. Allen was determined, as a letter he wrote to Kerouac indicates, that he was "no longer going to have homosexual affairs." (Miles, 125)

And for a while he did not. He met Helen Parker in Provincetown, Massachusetts. "Many of my fears and dun rags fell from me after the first night I slept with her, when we understood that we wanted each other and began a love affair." (Miles, 129) Older than Ginsberg, she had two boys, ages five and ten, had once been engaged to the novelist John Dos Passos, and had known Hemingway. She wanted Ginsberg to live with her and the children in Cape Cod and be father to them as well as husband to her. He could stay home and write, and she would support the family. Ginsberg could not see himself being a father. He wanted to continue with his therapy and to achieve his own financial independence. Their romance deteriorated; she left him for the folk singer, Ramblin' Jack Elliott. But Ginsberg had demonstrated to himself that he could be heterosexual, and that gratified him. He told Kerouac about it so enthusiastically that it appeared that much of his pleasure came from simply succeeding in being heterosexual and keeping homosexuality at bay.

Ginsberg did not feel the same shame about using drugs as

he did about being homosexual. He continued to smoke pot, which he did throughout his life, and in April 1952, while living with Louis and Edith in Paterson, he took peyote for the first time. He spent much of the day observing the details of the backyard garden and experiencing a consciousness of eternity. "I have been going around grinning idiotically at people— almost afraid they'll ask 'What's the matter with you …?'" he wrote. "But they seem to me also—so strange in their momentary consciousness." When "a piece of laundry dropped on the grass," and someone called out, "interrupting me in my observations of the world …—'Please Allen, will you hang that up?'"—his father was suddenly present and said, "He's busy with himself." (Ball, ed., *Journals* 9–10)

As always Ginsberg led a whirlwind social life. He spent much of his time in Greenwich Village at the San Remo Bar, the gathering place for avant-garde artists, poets, dancers, and theater people. He met and had an incoherent conversation with a drunken Dylan Thomas there. He also continued to see Kerouac, Carr, the poet Philip Lamantia, and Carl Solomon, now out of the hospital. In the winter of 1950, he met Gregory Corso, who became a lifelong friend. Abandoned as a kid, Corso had lived on the streets; a tough and a petty thief, he had been in and out of jails and mental hospitals most of his young life. When Ginsberg met him he was 20 and just out of jail. He showed Ginsburg some of his poems. Ginsberg liked them. He told Ginsberg how he was attracted by a girl who lived across the street from him; that he looked into her windows when she and her boyfriend made love. Ginsberg realized it was his friend, Dusty Moreland, and took Corso to meet her. Ginsberg treated women with the same regard as he did men and included them in his social and intellectual life. He berated Kerouac when Kerouac refused to see a woman Ginsberg wanted him to meet. Kerouac said he had nothing to learn from "girls," but only used them for sex.

In Paterson, Ginsberg got a job as a reporter on the *Labor Herald* through his uncle; he was fired after a few weeks. Then he worked at a ribbon factory picking up the broken threads and tying them back into the looms, but "my eyes unfocussed, I would daydream, I lost track of how to do the simplest things and wandered around embarrassedly trying to fit in." He was fired from that job, too, and complained to Cassady, "Truly the real world is my downfall." (Miles, 131) Actually he was adept at negotiating "the real world." Not only did he have his poem, "Pull My Daisy," published in a commercial magazine, but he was showing manuscripts by Kerouac and Burroughs as well as his own to publishers, and he landed both of them contracts at Ace Books, where Carl Solomon now worked. He wrote to Kerouac, "I am hung up on commerce with publishers: if I don't do it I know nothing would ever happen here. As soon as I establish everybody's position and reputation, will get on better kick. But all would die in

Naomi: Seeking Mother's Love

In his poem "Kaddish," Ginsberg recounts what it was like to be with Naomi when she came back home after one of her long hospital stays, particularly with regard to the frustration of love he experienced from her:

> She went to the bedroom to lie down in bed and ruminate, or nap, or hide—I went in with her, not leave her by herself—lay in bed next to her—shades pulled, dusky, late afternoon—Louis in front room at desk, waiting—perhaps boiling chicken for supper—'Don't be afraid of me because I'm just coming back home from the mental hospital—I'm your mother—'
> Poor love, lost—a fear—I lay there—Said. 'I love you Naomi,'— stiff; next to her arm. I would have cried, was this the comfortless lone union?—Nervous, and she got up soon.

NY if I weren't around to clean up messes. They're all in another world." (Schumacher, 142) Even as he continued to frequent the subterranean world of the San Remo, Ginsberg found a paying job doing market research, in December 1950, just the sort of thing that the poet Allen Ginsberg might deplore but would always be a master of.

IN THE WORLD

The summer of 1951, between jobs, Ginsberg accompanied Lucien Carr to Mexico City to visit Burroughs and Joan, where they went after Burroughs failed at pot farming and had been arrested for indecent behavior in Texas and drug possession in New Orleans. Burroughs was traveling through Latin America with a boyfriend searching for the drug, *yage*, when they arrived. Ginsberg and Carr spent time with Joan; then Ginsberg left for Texas. While he was in Texas, Ginsberg learned that after he returned, Burroughs had killed Joan when they were both quite drunk. Playing a fatal game of William Tell, Joan placed a glass on her head in lieu of an apple, Burroughs attempted to shoot it off, and, missing it, hit Joan. Burroughs pleaded guilty, but said the gun went off when he dropped it. He was released on bail, but before his trial fled to the United States.

Of all the influences that contributed to making Allen Ginsberg's poetry what it is, none was more important than William Carlos Williams. Williams was a champion of the American, as opposed to the British, in poetry, of the common voice as the measure of the verse line, of concrete and particular images from the populist world and the surrounding environment as the matter for verse. A physician, Williams worked with the poor, often without pay. Ginsberg saw him read at the Guggenheim Museum, then in Greenwich Village, on March 28, 1950, held back from approaching him after the reading, but two days later sent him this letter, parts of which Williams included in his long poem *Paterson*:

Dear Doctor:

In spite of the grey secrecy of time and my own self-shuttering doubts in these youthful rainy days, I would like to make my presence in Paterson known to you, and I hope you will welcome this from me, an unknown young poet, to you, an unknown old poet, who live in the same rusty county of the world....

I envision for myself some kind of new speech—different at least from what I have been writing down—in that it has to be clear statement of fact about misery (and not misery itself), and splendor if there is any out of the subjective wanderings through Paterson. This place is as I say my natural habitat by memory, and I am not following in your traces to be poetic: though I know you will be pleased to realize that at least one actual citizen of your community has inherited your experience in his struggle to love and know his own world-city, through your work.... I may need a new measure myself, but though I have a flair for your style I seldom dig exactly what you are doing with cadences, line length, sometimes syntax, etc., and cannot handle your work as a solid object—which properties I assume you rightly claim. I don't understand the measure. I haven't worked with it much either, though, which must make the difference. But I would like to talk with you concretely on this.... (Schumacher, 123)

Williams recognized a new voice and a kindred sensibility. He was less taken by the poems Ginsberg included, nor were they representative of the kind of poetry Williams wrote or Ginsberg described. Rhymed and metrical, Williams found them imperfect. He told Ginsberg, "In this mode, perfection is basic." But, like Williams, Ginsberg was not trying to master that form. "I have to learn how to talk naturally in verse," Ginsberg wrote Kerouac," find out how to say great things or beautiful things naturally." (Miles, 145) He found that natural voice in the sketches he had been entering in his notebooks, drawing in words whatever caught his eye, the way painters make studies in pencil.

Early in 1952, Ginsberg went through his notebooks, selected a group of prose sketches, rearranged the lines of the paragraphs according to breath durations, and set them on the page in triplets so that they looked like poetry. He sent them to Williams, saying they were "fragmentary notes I picked out of a journal and put in lines just as an experiment about a year ago. I gave them up, thinking they were nothing, thinking also that I was aimlessly trying to make poetry out of prose scraps." (Miles, 144) Detractors would jump to agree. But Williams wrote back that they were "wonderful.... How many of such poems as these do you own? You *must* have a book, I shall see that you get it. Don't throw anything away. These are *it.*" Ginsberg wrote Kerouac and Cassady, "Now you realize, you old bonepoles, the two of you, whuzzat means? I can get a book out if I want." Typically, he added, he hoped to get their work published, too. (Schumacher, 140)

He dug through his journals, assembled more poems, and sent them to Williams. Williams rejected a number of them to make a "lean, strong" book of 47 poems, *Empty Mirror.* Even with Williams's backing, the book was not published until 1961—after Ginsberg had become famous.

Ginsberg and Williams became friends and Ginsberg took him through parts of Paterson he had forgotten or had not known. The encounter with Williams helped Ginsberg not only to begin to find his own poetic voice but to refine a sensibility that could make him, as Coleridge called it, an Aeolian harp, the medium through which the winds of the world blow and become transformed into poetry.

Ginsberg's life was becoming steady and balanced. He was finding himself, and learning what he wanted to do, but many of his friends were floundering. Dusty Moreland, with whom Ginsberg was living in a small New York apartment, was depressed over her cat's death and hard to get along with. Carl Solomon had gone on a binge for two weeks, stabbed his books, thrown paint around his apartment, screamed in the street, and been in and out of Bellevue. On June 12, 1952, Ginsberg wrote Burroughs that his life was "getting out of hand with your going off after your own kind of Mobydick, Carl crazy, Jack nutty as a fruitcake. Everybody seems off their heads, blowing tops around me." An example of Kerouac's temper came a few months later. Frustrated that his books were not being published and that his friend John Clellon Holmes's novel, *Go*—which used much the same material as *On the Road*—had been and had brought Holmes $20,000 for the paperback rights, Kerouac wrote Ginsberg a letter attacking all his friends and accusing Ginsberg of jealousy and of trying to sabotage his career. Ginsberg waited out the storm, and a month later, Kerouac sent him an affectionate conciliatory letter along with the manuscript of *Dr. Sax*, which he hoped Ginsberg could place with a publisher. In his June letter to Burroughs, Ginsberg concluded, "I don't have a moment's peace from these people with their cats and yages [the hallucinogen Burroughs had found in South America] and wives and voids and angers at the universe, why can't everybody calm down, I always say, like the nice people in the boobyhatch." (Schumacher, 148) The passage shows once again that despite his own seeming craziness, Ginsberg always was blessed with calm, comic perspective, whether when expelled from school, in the "boobyhatch," or taking peyote in his parents' house. He knew himself and his tendency, which

> Lucien warn[ed] me against the other day … to drift off into unreality of thought to place where I met Carl—Madhouse.… I must abandon again this whole metaphysical urge that leads me further each month back to an uncreated world of bliss of my own making in my own head … while the real world passes me by. (Ball, ed., *Journals* 25)

Ginsberg ended this journal entry with a list of resolutions: to get his own apartment, and a job, "*any* kind … maybe totally non-literary," to "stop playing with my mind, with my life," and to "*make*" something "happen to my life."

Ginsberg also complained in this entry that he had no "place in society. I have no function in the world I live in." Necessary as carving out that place was, the development of a world more welcoming was also essential. It had to become open, even vulnerable to what he had to offer. And cracks in the culture were starting to show, in part because of the kind of life the Beat writers were living and which the mass media were beginning to popularize by reporting it. An indigenous folk culture along with and prodded by the Beats was emerging because of opposition to the Cold War, repressive puritanism, conformity, racial brutality, and mass, consumer culture.

In 1953, Ginsberg began studying Chinese art in the reading room of the Forty-Second Street Library in New York, looking at reproductions. In order to understand them better, he began to read Eastern philosophy and came upon D.T. Suzuki's *Introduction to Zen Buddhism*. It led him to pay attention to his imagination as well as to the details and contours of the outer world. "Sakyamuni Coming Out from the Mountain," which Ginsberg wrote after looking at a 12th-century Chinese scroll painting of that name by Liang-Kai, "recounts the exhaustion that a holy man, possibly Buddha in one of his forms, feels after seeking enlightenment, only to experience satori when 'he realized/the land of blessedness exists/in the imagination.'" (Schumacher, 153) Using an ancient Chinese mask, Ginsberg represented his own condition and the direction of his poetry. Ginsberg wrote Neal Cassady,

> I discover life so unsatisfactory that I am beginning to use my imagination … to invent alternatives…. For … (imagination) seems to me in my state present to be my temporary only value salvation and Good." (Schumacher, 154)

After "Sakyamuni," Ginsberg wrote "The Green Automobile," which he called his "first breakthrough as a poet." For the "first time," he wrote, "I let my imagination and desire dominate over what, in the mental hospital, I had been taught to accept as an adjustment to reality, to limit my demands of the external world to what could be workable so as to avoid excess suffering." (Miles, 153) In "The Green Automobile," he openly expressed his love for Neal Cassady by recreating it as "a legend," he wrote to Cassady, "of my poor sad summer with you." But rather than a complaint and an expression of negation and despair as his "Denver Doldrums" had been, Ginsberg tried "to create some recognizable human-angelic ideal story." (Miles, 154) He was freeing himself from denigrating and denying his homosexuality.

Towards the end of the summer of 1953—Ginsberg was working as a copyboy at *The New York World Telegram and Sun*—Burroughs arrived in New York—having jumped bail in Mexico—and moved in with Ginsberg and Gregory Corso. Ginsberg and Burroughs had not seen each other for six years. They clicked. "He is really exciting to talk to," Ginsberg wrote Cassady, more so for me than ever. His new loquaciousness is something I never had the advantage of. I'm older now and the emotional relationship and conflict of will and mutual digging are very intense, continuous, exhausting and fertile.... One of the deepest people I ever saw. (Miles, 155) He is very great, greater than I ever realized. (Schumacher, 157)

In a reversal of Ginsberg's situation with Cassady, Burroughs fell in love with Ginsberg. Although not sexually attracted to him, Ginsberg loved Burroughs and "saw the soft center where [Burroughs] felt isolated, alone in the world and [that] he needed ... a feeling of affection," and, in consequence, he did have sex with him. Burroughs was in New York on his way to Tangiers, and tried to persuade Ginsberg to go with him. But Ginsberg did not want to make their sexual involvement permanent. When he crudely told Burroughs he did not find him sexually exciting, "it wounded [Burroughs] terribly because it was like complete physical rejection in a way I didn't mean. Like a heart blow that severed the trust, because I'd freaked out for that moment, and regretted it ever since." (Miles, 156)

In December 1953, Burroughs set out for Tangiers by boat. Ginsberg gave up his apartment, borrowed money from his brother and friends, collected back pay from the *Telegram,* sold his refrigerator, and set off for the Yucatan to see ancient Mayan ruins. He wrote Cassady that he needed to take time away from "NYC intellectual beauties" to experience the "manly savage solitude of jungles." (Miles, 156)

Like Ulysses, Ginsberg was a man who was never at a loss. By the time he went to explore the jungle of the Yucatan he had explored the jungle of the city, the jungle of his own consciousness, the jungle of the madhouse, and the jungle of the subterranean world, and in each case he had survived his journeys to these dark centers and returned with increased power.

Arriving in Mérida on December 31, 1953, he celebrated New Year's Eve at a country club party, noting in his diary that he felt awkward without a tuxedo. Two days later he set off for the Mayan ruins of Chichén Itza. Before leaving New York City he had obtained a pass from a friend at the Museum of Natural History allowing him to stay without charge at archeological sites. The first night in Chichén Itza, he climbed to the top of the pyramid of El Castillo, a Mayan temple dating from the 11th century, stretched a hammock, took some paracodin, looked at the stars, listened to the sounds of birds and insects, and began to write "Siesta in Xbalba." Several days later, he traveled to the Uxmal ruins, a group of palaces that had recently been excavated. From there he went to Chiapas and met Karena Shields, a writer of jungle fiction for children and of scholarly papers on archeology. She ran a cocoa plantation. Twenty years earlier she had played Jane in Tarzan movies. The region of Chiapas where her plantation was located, Xibalba, according to Mayan mythology, was the site of purgatory. Ginsberg stayed with Shields, explored the region on horseback, waded in the streams, read the Christian gospels, Thomas Merton's *The Seven Story Mountain*, the writings of 14th-century Catholic mystics, and built a set of drums made out of logs.

After nearly six months in Mexico, with the help of a loan from Karena Shields, Ginsberg left for California to stay with Neal and Carolyn Cassady. It was a replay of Denver. Ginsberg pined for Neal, Neal was cold, the scant sexual contact they did have lacked emotional connection, and Carolyn finally caught them in bed together. She forbade Ginsberg to ever see Neal again, drove him to Berkeley, and gave him $20.

chapter
five

Fame

Bliss was it in that dawn to be alive
But to be young was very heaven.
> —William Wordsworth, *The Prelude*

SAN FRANCISCO

Arriving in San Francisco, broke and on borrowed money, Ginsberg took a six- dollar-a-week room in a small hotel run by a lesbian couple. In the early 1950s San Francisco was a haven for Bohemians whose values and lifestyles alienated them from mainstream America. Anarchists, ecologists, poets, jazz musicians, Abstract Expressionist painters, intellectuals, actors in experimental theater companies, atheists, and Buddhists lived together and nourished each other. At the heart of the San Francisco scene was North Beach with its bars, street life, and two local culture centers—a small paperback bookstore run by Lawrence Ferlinghetti called City Lights and an old automobile repair shop converted by six experimentalist painters into an art gallery/performance space, The Six Gallery.

In San Francisco, Ginsberg met Sheila Boucher, a young divorcee with "a wild mind" and a four-year-old son. "Finer than *any* girl I met," Ginsberg wrote, and after a few weeks he moved in with her and found a job doing market research. Sheila had sung in small nightspots. When Ginsberg met her, she was an advertising copywriter. Ginsberg did not tell her about his bisexuality, but Neal Cassady was making frequent trips to San Francisco, his marriage was on the rocks again, he was smoking a lot of dope, sleeping around, and hanging Ginsberg up with his old pattern of seduction and rejection. And Ginsberg's relationship with Burroughs was still murky. Back in New York from Tangiers, Burroughs was planning to come to San Francisco. Ginsberg had told him about Sheila, but had not clearly and definitely rejected a sexual relationship with him. Burroughs wrote Kerouac that he would only visit Ginsberg if their sexual relationship resumed. Kerouac wrote Ginsberg that they all ought "to return to Beat Generation 1947 confessions & honesties." (Schumacher, 186) Ginsberg's psychotherapist gave similar advice. In an attempt to clear away confusion,

Ginsberg wrote Burroughs that he did not want a sexual connection with him. Burroughs cancelled his plans to go to San Francisco and sailed back to Tangiers. Then Ginsberg told Sheila of his love affair with Neal Cassady; she hit the ceiling and refused to sleep with him. Tension and bickering ensued until one night after a bitter fight, Ginsberg roamed the San Francisco streets. Unable to get drunk, he stopped into Forster's Cafeteria, where artists hung out, and struck up a conversation with Robert LaVigne, a young painter. After some talk about the New York art scene, LaVigne invited Ginsberg back to his place to see his paintings.

Several of the paintings were studies of the same young man. Moved by his physical beauty and facial expression, Ginsberg asked who the model was. LaVigne told him it was Peter Orlovsky, who lived with him. At that moment, Orlovsky walked in. He was a delicate but resilient creature, one of five children. His father had failed in business, taken to drink, and become brutal. His mother, deaf and with partially paralyzed facial muscles, also was alcoholic. Ultimately she took the children, left her husband, and lived in poverty. Before Orlovsky had finished high school, she looked him over, told him, "You're a big, handsome boy with strong hands. You'll have no difficulty getting jobs in your life," and turned him out of the house. For three years he worked at depressing, menial jobs, caring for senile patients in a mental hospital and mopping floors. In 1953, he was drafted for the Korean War. When a lieutenant saw him reading Erich Fromm's *Escape from Freedom*, he asked him if he were a Communist. Orlovsky replied, "An army is an army against love." He was sent to spend the rest of his time in the military working as a medic in an army hospital in San Francisco.

LaVigne met him during this period when on his days off Orlovsky took long walks. LaVigne offered companionship. "I was very scared," Orlovsky said of himself at the time he met LaVigne. "I was young. I've always liked girls, but I couldn't make it with them yet. I didn't know how to do it. I was … a hermit…. I was going to spend the rest of my life by myself unless I had a brainstorm. But Bob LaVigne came along and there was a whole new friendship, exciting sexual knowledge…." (Miles, 182) When Ginsberg and Orlovsky met, Peter's affair with LaVigne was ending. Sensing Orlovsky's delicacy, Ginsberg approached him gently, and it was Orlovsky who first embraced Ginsberg. Their first night together was passed without overt sexual contact. Nevertheless, the kinds of emotional turmoil, confusion, and jealousy that accompany the ends and the beginnings of love affairs arose for LaVigne, Ginsberg, and Orlovsky. After several weeks of melodrama, they all took rooms by themselves. Ginsberg was unhappy and confused. He had been moved by his loving encounter with Orlovsky, but he was unsure about committing himself to a homosexual relationship and he was worried about the future. He spoke to the psychotherapist he was seeing:

> I said that I was dissatisfied with what I was doing, I was very unsure of myself. So he said, "What would you like to do? What is your desire, really?" I said, "Doctor, I don't think you're going to find this very healthy and clear but I really would like to stop working forever—never work again, never do anything like the kind of work I'm doing now— and do nothing but write poetry and have leisure to spend the day outdoors and to go to museums and see friends. And I'd like to keep living with someone—maybe even a man— and explore relationships that way…." Then *he* said, "Well, why don't you? … If that is what you really feel would please you, what in the world is stopping you from doing it?" … I said the only thing stopping me was … feeling that that kind

of screwy thinking wasn't exactly contributing toward my general development, and he said that it obviously was contributing toward *something*, if it was what I wanted to do with my life. (Kramer, "Paterfamilias—I"54)

The exchange was catalyzing. Within a few weeks Ginsberg and Orlovsky moved in together and established a bond that lasted the rest of their lives. They made a formal commitment to each other with marriage vows at Forster's Cafeteria in February 1955:

> We held hands, took a vow: I do, I do, you promise? yes, I do. At that instant we looked in each other's eyes and there was a kind of celestial cold fire that crept over us and blazed up and illuminated the entire cafeteria and made it an eternal place.
>
> I found somebody who'd accept my devotion, and he found somebody who'd accept his devotion and who was devoted to him. It was really a fulfillment of a fantasy, to a point where fantasy and reality finally merged. Desire illuminated the room, because it was a fulfillment of all my fantasies since I was nine, when I began to have erotic love fantasies. And that vow has stuck as the primary core of our relationship.... It's really the basic human relationship—you give yourself to each other, help each other and don't go to heaven without each other. (Schumacher, 193)

Regarding work, Ginsberg figured out that a computer could replace him at Towne-Oller and save the company money to boot. He took the plan to his bosses and they gratefully laid him off with a statement to the unemployment bureau that Ginsberg was a victim of technological progress. He collected unemployment insurance for half a year.

The commitment Ginsberg and Orlovsky made to each other did not make their relationship easier. Orlovsky was moody and mercurial with a precarious mental balance, like Ginsberg's mother. He thought of himself, moreover, as primarily heterosexual, and was homosexual only out of devotion to Ginsberg. Throughout their years together, Orlovsky experienced serious episodes of instability, sometimes passing into realms beyond sanity and sometimes addicted to destructive drugs like speed. Sometimes, too, he expressed sexual alienation from Ginsberg and they slept separately, as in the spring of 1955. That June, too, Orlovsky hitchhiked back to New York and returned with his 15-year-old brother, Lafcadio, who was on the verge of mental breakdown, Orlovsky's two older brothers were catatonic and confined to a mental hospital.

While Orlovsky was away, Ginsberg learned that Carl Solomon was in Pilgrim State Hospital again and began writing "Howl," trying to write spontaneously in Kerouac's style, using long lines to plow deep into the places of pain he and his friends had known. Although she is not ostensibly the subject, it is a poem about his mother, too:

> I realized after I wrote it that it was addressed to her.... "Howl" is actually to her rather than to Carl in a sense. Because the emotion that comes from it is built on my mother, not on anything as superficial as a later acquaintance, such as Carl. (Schumacher, 208)

When Orlovsky returned with Lafcadio, Ginsberg's solitary poet's life was disrupted. Having Lafcadio in the house seemed "like being married & having an overgrown problem child." (Schumacher, 205) Ginsberg rented a one-room cottage in Berkeley, a few blocks away from the university, where he was a graduate student. He continued to work on "Howl" and wrote

"A Strange New Cottage in Berkeley" about practical work and the nourishment that comes from it and the phantasmagorical comic tribute to Walt Whitman in which he takes his place as Whitman's heir, "A Supermarket in California."

At a reading by W.H. Auden, Ginsberg met Michael McClure, a San Francisco poet who told him he had been asked to organize a reading of new poets at the Six Gallery and added that he did not have the time to do it. Ginsberg said he would. Through Kenneth Rexroth, the poet anarchist at the center of the San Francisco poetry scene, Ginsberg got the names of several poets, among them Gary Snyder. Ginsberg and Snyder immediately took a liking to each other. Both shared an interest in Buddhism and admired William Carlos Williams. In addition to Snyder, Ginsberg asked Philip Lamantia, Michael McClure, and Philip Whalen to read. Rexroth introduced the proceedings and the poets. Kerouac declined to read, but roamed about the audience with a jug of wine, freely offering it. When Ginsberg read "Howl," he kept up a steady stream of encouragement, like a jazz aficionado, calling out "Go," throughout the reading. By the end, Ginsberg was in tears, so was Rexroth, and the overflowing crowd exploded with excitement. It was poetry as poetry had not been presented, a visceral expedition into the culture and consciousness of a living present. After the reading, Kerouac told Ginsberg that "Howl" would make him famous in San Francisco. Rexroth amended it. "This poem will make you famous from bridge to bridge." But even that assessment was too cautious. "Howl" gave Ginsberg worldwide recognition and a career as a poet, a prophet, a teacher, and a catalyst for revolutionary changes in consciousness and culture for the rest of his life. In the morning, Ferlinghetti telegrammed: "I greet you at the beginning of a great career. When do I get the manuscript?" (Schumacher, 216)

Ferlighetti had started publishing pamphlet-size poetry books in The Pocket Poets Series. *Howl*, published in August 1956, was the fourth number. Ginsberg filled out the volume with his raucous, comic, angry "America," "A Supermarket in California," "Sunflower Sutra," a meditation on the decay of the flesh and the transcendental beauty of the spirit, and with several earlier poems. Ferlinghetti asked William Carlos Williams to write the introduction, and he did, ending it with an implicit comparison of Ginsberg to Dante with the warning, "Hold back the edges of your gowns, Ladies, we are going through hell."

By the time of *Howl*'s publication, Ginsberg and the San Francisco scene were nationally known. The editor of *The New York Times Sunday Book Review* sent the poet Richard Eberhart to San Francisco to write about what Rexroth called the poetry renaissance. Ginsberg, savvy as ever about marketing, guided him around the city and introduced him to the poets and explained the scene. "West Coast Rhythms" appeared in the Book Review September 2, 1956, a month after the publication of "Howl." Eberhart wrote that "the West Coast is the liveliest spot in the country in poetry," (Schumacher, 228) that there was a "new vital group consciousness now among young poets in the Bay region…. They have exuberance and a young will to kick down the doors of older consciousness and established practice in favor of what they think is vital and new." (Schumacher, 240) Ginsberg, he wrote, possessed a "spiritual quality," had "a grasp of significance beyond real things." (Schumacher, 228) He wrote that "Howl" was "the most remarkable poem of the … group…. It is," Eberhart continued,

a howl against everything in our mechanistic civilization which kills the spirit…. It lays bare the nerves of suffering a spiritual struggle. Its positive force and energy come from a

redemptive quality of love, although it destructively cata-
logues evils of our time from physical deprivation to
madness. (Schumacher, 239)

Both *Life* and *Mademoiselle* did photo essays on the San

New York Subterranea: The Early 1950s

There was a strong avant-garde Bohemian art scene in New
York City in the 1950s. Ginsberg met many of the artists who
composed this circle at the San Remo Bar in Greenwich Village,
on the northwest corner of Bleecker and MacDougal Streets.
Their work appeared in little magazines, in small galleries, and
in theaters located off-Broadway before "off-Broadway" became
a chic designation. The artists who formed this circle were dedicated to exploring the psychology of perception, of liberating art
forms from linearity and even narrative coherence, of being critical of what seemed like acceptable routines. They were also
dedicated to existing outside the cultural and economic establishment, believing if they were independent of corporate
financing or the taste of audiences conditioned by mass-culture
they could form a community of artists that might live closer to
the truth and develop an art more authentic and truthful than
the art of the dominant culture.

Living closer to the truth, for many, meant being able to live
sexual lives that defied conventional taboos. Many of the
artists—for example, the modern dance pioneer Merce Cun-
ningham and his collaborator, the avant-garde composer John
Cage—were homosexual. Many others were bisexual, including
anarchist pacifist novelist, poet, and social critic Paul Goodman
and anarchist pacifist actor, director, painter, and The Living Theater cofounder Julian Beck.

This was the milieu of which Ginsberg became part, making
lifelong friends and associates after he was released from the
Columbia Psychiatric Institute.

Francisco poets, *Esquire* and *Mademoiselle* published poems by Ginsberg, and Ginsberg was invited to be the guest editor for issues of *The Black Mountain Review* and *The Evergreen Review*, giving him the opportunity to publish Kerouac, Corso, Burroughs, and other friends. In New York, Ginsberg tirelessly went to literary parties and promoted Beat and Bay area writers, and gave interviews to *The New York Times*, *The World Telegram and Sun*, and *The Village Voice*. But the best publicity was yet to come. There was a harbinger of it when Ferlinghetti's printers in England warned there might be difficulty getting the book past the censors in the United States Customs Department. Ferlinghetti contacted the American Civil Liberties Union in case he might need legal assistance, and Ginsberg wrote to his father, "I am ready to tackle the U.S. Govt out of sheer self delight." (Schumacher, ed., *Family Business* 39)

In October 1956, the first printing of *Howl* passed through customs. The second printing was confiscated in March 1957. On April 3, the American Civil Liberties Union challenged the legality of the seizure, on May 19, *The San Francisco Chronicle* gave Ferlinghetti space in the paper to write a defense of the poem, and on May 29, advised by a Washington, D.C customs official not to take action against *Howl*, the U.S. Attorney in San Francisco released the confiscated copies. But that was not the end. On May 21, a week before the second printing was released, two plainclothes policemen bought a copy of *Howl* at The City Lights Bookstore. Subsequently, Ferlinghetti and the clerk at City Lights who sold the book were arrested. They faced six months in jail and $500 fines. Their trial began on August 22, 1957, garnered immense media attention, and in October, Judge Clayton W. Horn, a Sunday school Bible teacher, ruled in favor of the poem.

Ginsberg himself did not appear at the trial. In June 1956, he had signed on to voyage to the Arctic as a yeoman storekeeper on a the mission to deliver supplies to the contingent stationed there running the Distant Early Warning System, one of the mechanisms of the Cold War. Its function was to detect nuclear missiles fired from the Soviet Union at the United States. Ironic though it was that the poet of "Howl" should do such work, Ginsberg wanted to make fast money for a trip to Tangiers and Europe, and going to sea allowed him to save a thousand dollars. Perhaps it was also a way of getting back to himself and not drowning in newfound fame. A few days before his departure, he learned in a telegram that his brother Gene sent to Orlovsky—thinking that Allen had already shipped out—that Naomi had died. Ginsberg did not go to her funeral. It was small and there were not enough men to make a *minyan*—the requisite group of 10 Jewish men required for a prayer service—so the prayer for the dead, the Kaddish, could not be recited for Naomi. Allen began to mull one over in his mind, but it would not become fully realized for several years.

Ginsberg returned from sea in September. In November, with Orlovsky, Orlovsky's brother Lafcadio, and Gregory Corso, he arrived in Mexico to visit Kerouac for two weeks. From there Ginsberg, Kerouac, and the Orlovskys drove to New York. In February, Kerouac sailed for Tangiers to see Burroughs, and on March 8, Ginsberg and Orlovsky followed.

ABROAD

Kerouac left Tangiers soon after Ginsberg and Orlovsky arrived. In June, Ginsberg and Orlovsky left for Spain. Burroughs had kicked his morphine habit and was writing drafts of *Naked Lunch*. The manuscript was massive and disorganized, and Ginsberg worked with him editing it into the book it became. Despite Burroughs's assurances that he would not be sexually demanding or jealous, he was—using his caustic intelligence to make Orlovsky uncomfortable. Ginsberg got angry, and even cut Burroughs shirt during one blowup.

Ginsberg and Orlovsky stopped in the great Spanish cities—Granada, Seville, Cordoba, Madrid, Barcelona—and looked at the antiquities and the architecture, went to the museums, and looked at how people lived. They crossed over into France, hitchhiked to Venice, arrived in July, and stayed until September, making side trips to Florence, Rome, Assisi, and Naples. Ginsberg was exuberant about the "classical openness" of Florence, "the spot where all the medieval stiffness and religious fear gave way and Renaissance burst through with huge naked idealized human bodies." (Schumacher, 265) He was outraged, however, "to go into the Vatican and see them desecrating the very significance and point of ancient sculpture" by covering the naked forms with fig leaves or painted on drapery, as in Michelangelo's *Last Judgement.* "It stands out like the piece of dirtymindedness that it is." (Schumacher, 265) He was also disappointed by the monks in Assisi: "I got the impression they'd be bugged by St. Francis ... if he reappeared on the streets of Assisi in his tattered cloak, begging and singing ... like he used to." (Schumacher, 266) Ginsberg was no less disappointed by his meeting with the poet W.H. Auden on the isle of Ischia off the coast of Naples. They argued about politics and poetry, Auden taking conservative positions on capital punishment and censorship, expressing dislike for Shelley and Whitman, and dismissing "Howl" as self-pitying. (Shumacher, 268)

After these peregrinations, Ginsberg returned to Paris and moved into a room he shared with Orlovsky and Gregory Corso at a cheap, rundown hotel in the Bohemian quarter. "Paris," he wrote,

is beautiful, the only city I've seen so far that would tempt me to expatriate and settle down. The rest of Europe has been interesting, and each city has its one, two or three marvels or charms, but Paris has universal interest and permanent charm as a living place.... [F]aces on the street look like they've stepped out of paintings by Lautrec and Van Gogh ... streets look like impressionist streets. (Schumacher, 270)

Ginsberg had brought the manuscript of *Naked Lunch* with him, and tried to place it with The Olympia Press, famous for publishing literary works other publishers would avoid—like Henry Miller's novels—but was turned down. He also was intent on pursuing his own writing, and the work he began in Paris reflects his characteristic focus on both personal and social/political experience. One event stirring him was Naomi's death. At the café *Le Select*, he started noting down all the images of his mother that he could gather, and he tried to imagine how the world looked to her. This was the start of "Kaddish."

The other event capturing his imagination was the launching of the space satellite *Sputnik* by the Soviet Union, in the fall of 1957. Not only did it give Russia a big jump on the United States in the Cold War arms race and a propaganda victory regarding the advances that had been made in the Soviet Union since the revolution of 1917, but it suggested to Ginsberg that the values of the Beat generation were not as far-fetched as they had been depicted by mainstream opinion. He wrote to his father:

People keep seeing destruction or rebellion [in Beat literature] ... but that is [a] very minor element, actually; it only seems to be so to people who have accepted standard American values as permanent. What we are saying is that these values are not really standard or permanent, and we are in a sense I think ahead of the times—though not too far ahead. Sputnik has already changed the content of the editorial pages I read.... Whitman long ago complained that unless the material power of America were leavened by some kind of spiritual infusion we would wind up among the 'fabled damned.' It seems we're approaching that state as far as I can see. Only way out is individuals taking responsibility and saying what they actually feel—which is an enormous human achievement in any society. That's just what we as a 'group' have been trying to do. (Schumacher, 273)

Kerouac wanted Ginsberg to "ignore war, ignore politics, ignore" injustice in his writing. Ginsberg chose rather to ignore that advice: "I'd like to write a monstrous and golden political or historical poem about the fall of America," he had written to Kerouac. "If poetry can be made of ashcans why not newspaper headlines and politics?" (Schumacher, 276) It was more than a question. It became his poetic credo. It is nearly impossible to see the dividing line between personal and political experience, between private and social responses in his poetry, whether he was writing about the plight of his mother, the plight of America, or the plight of the human spirit.

Orlovsky left Paris before Ginsberg to deal with recurring family crises, and Burroughs came to Paris, calmer than he had been in Tangiers, no longer insistent and needy, and his relationship with Ginsberg deepened. During this period, too, Ginsberg saw the beginning of his celebrity, was interviewed by Art Buchwald of *The Herald-Tribune*, met American film director John Huston, and a number of international luminaries, the French novelist Louis-Ferdinand Celine, Tristan Tzara, the Dadaist poet, the photographer Man Ray, and Marcel Duchamps, creator of surrealist paintings and installations. He was invited to London twice to read and record his poetry for the BBC. He and Corso had lunch with the poet Edith Sitwell at her club. She told them she liked their work, but declined their invitation that she try heroin or pose in the nude for an anthology of naked poets. Ginsberg's meeting with Auden this time was collegial and Auden even expressed appreciation for his poetry. (Miles, 242, 244)

Poet/Activist

Vietnam War flesh-heap grows higher
blood splashing down the mountains of bodies
on to Cholon's sidewalks
                        —Allen Ginsberg, "Crossing Nation"

TRANSITIONS AND DISCOVERIES

When he returned to the United States in the fall of 1958, Ginsberg took an apartment with Orlovsky on the Lower East Side of Manhattan. Ginsberg wanted to have a place free from the commotion of his Paris hotel room, where he could work without a continuous stream of friends passing through. Life in New York proved to be busier, however, and more hectic than life in Paris. It was a chaotic and tumultuous time in America and momentous changes were beginning. Ginsberg, as always, was partly directing them, and constantly on the go, his life defined by an unnerving quest to create himself through self obliteration whether by visions, sex, drugs, madness, or chanting. This project of self-definition, of becoming pure awareness, and of carrying out his poetic vocation was never separate, either, from his radical, even messianic social involvement and political activity. As usual, too, he provided a fixed center, despite whatever turbulence he was undergoing, for a number of other people.

Sheila Boucher, whom Ginsberg had lived with in San Francisco, had hitchhiked to New York with her lover (fleeing a husband) and needed a place to stay. Robert LaVigne, who had introduced Ginsberg to Orlovsky, was also in New York and stayed with them. So did Carl Solomon, just released from Pilgrim State Hospital.

Neal Cassady, in California, had been sentenced to five years in San Quentin for giving two joints of marijuana to undercover cops. Carolyn wrote Ginsberg asking for help. Kerouac, now famous for *On the Road*, was bitter about the transformation of the Beat ideal into a pop culture commodity and about the poor reception of his other work. Alcoholic, he often lashed out at Ginsberg. Kerouac's bigoted mother, who despised Jews and reported Ginsberg and Burroughs to the F.B.I. as "dope fiends," forbade Jack to see Ginsberg, intercepted Ginsberg's phone calls, opened his letters, and wrote telling him to stay away. Kerouac excused his mother, shared many of her bigotries, and periodically did, in fact, stop seeing Ginsberg. (Ginsberg, nevertheless, kept writing and calling him, and there were still periods when Kerouac came to the city and spent time with Ginsberg, although it might be when he barged in drunk, raucous, uninvited, and at 4:00 A.M.). Peter Orlovsky was renewing his relationship with his father, with whom he had been rooming while Ginsberg was in Paris. Orlovsky was also keeping his mother from having his brother, Lafcadio, lobotomized; Lafcadio believed Martians were coming to rescue him from Earth. Orlovsky also fought and frequently succumbed to his own demons, suffering fits of violent behavior, often directed against himself, compulsive hypercleanliness, alcoholism, and methedrine (speed) addiction for the rest of his life.

Not long after the vindication of "Howl," in the fall of 1958, the trustees of the University of Chicago stopped the editors of *The Chicago Review* from publishing a section of Burroughs's *Naked Lunch.* The entire board, but for one member, resigned and started the little magazine *Big Table,* in which they printed the banned writing. On January 29, Ginsberg and Corso gave a benefit reading for *Big Table* in Chicago, brought out a huge crowd and generated front-page newspaper coverage and features in national magazines.

In mid-January, Ginsberg did a benefit poetry reading for The Living Theater to raise money for a production of William Carlos Williams's play *Many Loves.* In April, with several remunerative invitations to read his poetry, Ginsberg flew to San Francisco and also did benefits for several little magazines published by some of the Bay area poets. Before leaving New York, he persuaded a reluctant Kerouac, now comfortable from the sales of *On the Road,* to give him enough money to buy Neal Cassady a typewriter for his creative writing class in San

Quentin. Ginsberg visited Cassady in prison, delivered the typewriter, and gave a reading of "Kaddish" to enthusiastic prisoners.

Ginsberg's travels, performances, and communal hospitality did not keep him from making the New York social scene at the San Remo, the Cedar Tavern, or the Five Spot—where he got to know Thelonius Monk—or from continuing to write and perform. He played himself in the underground Beat movie, *Pull My Daisy,* wrote a review of Kerouac's books in *The Village Voice*, and published the essay, "Poetry, Violence, and The Trembling Lambs," in *The San Francisco Chronicle* in July. In that essay, he asserted the connection between poetry and the radical social criticism that defined his world view for the rest of his life—denouncing the money system, war, sexual repression, conformity, authoritarianism, and materialist consciousness. He gave interviews, showed his friends' manuscripts to publishers, coedited magazines, and kept writing poetry. He completed "Kaddish," after a Friday night spent listening to Ray Charles records, reading Shelley's "Adonais"—the

Explorer

During Ginsberg's stay in Mexico, a series of tremors shook the earth. Rumors spread that Yajalon, a nearby mountain village, had been destroyed by the volcano Acavalna. Ginsberg got a ride to Yajalon in a biplane and found the village hardly affected. Along with several villagers, Ginsberg set out to see if the volcano was active. They climbed to the top of the dormant volcano. The village elders sent a report of Ginsberg's findings to the Mexican Geological Institute. For leading the expedition, Ginsberg was acclaimed a hero by the villagers and was asked to lead another expedition with villagers to explore a legendary mountain cave.

elegy on the death of Keats—and hearing his friend Zev Put-
terman chant the Aramaic Mourner's Kaddish said by bereaved
Jews, staying up all weekend sustained by coffee, boiled eggs
that Orlovsky brought him, and Dexedrine.

One of the most important events of 1959 for Ginsberg, and
perhaps the most personally significant, was a reading at
Columbia University in February, attended by more than 1,400
people. Describing the reading to Ferlinghetti, Ginsberg wrote:

> It's my old school I was kicked out of so I suppose I'm hung
> up on making it there and breaking its reactionary back.... I
> almost went mad on the stage weeping over ... "Kaddish,"
> and my Pop in the audience[,] and denouncing the English
> faculty as a pack of ignorant amateurs. Gave long lecture on
> Prosody etc and we answered questions ... Strange night....
> God, reporters all over, all asking the same questions and no
> end in sight, it's getting stranger and stranger, life. Beginning
> to get invites from TV programs. (Miles, 260)

On one of them early in 1961, a Sunday night talk show hosted
by *Herald Tribune* television columnist John Crosby, Ginsberg
spoke of the virtues of marijuana, and the F.B.I. began what
would become a large file on him.

Ginsberg had always used drugs to derange his senses,
deepen consciousness, stimulate mental images, and excite
breath rhythms. While he was in California in the spring of
1959 he participated, at the invitation of Gregory Bateson, the
psychologist and anthropologist, in experiments with the hallucinogen, LSD. He wrote his father, LSD was "astounding....
went into ... a fantasy much like Coleridge World of Kubla
Kahn, saw a vision of that part of my consciousness which
seemed to be permanent and transcendent and identical with
the origin of the universe.... This drug," he concluded, "seems

automatically to produce a mystical experience. Science is getting very hip." (Schumacher, ed., *Family Business* 121–122) Soon afterwards, he met Timothy Leary, who had just begun working with LSD at Harvard, where he taught. Ginsberg became convinced of the beneficial effects of LSD for the expansion of individual consciousness and the creation of a peaceful and loving society and became an active proselytizer for it.

Between his first experience of LSD with Bateson and his taking psilocybin with Leary, Ginsberg experimented with yage, a hallucinogen that Burroughs had recommended for penetrating to and transcending the depths of consciousness. For Ginsberg, it was a near death experience. He was in South America for a writers' conference sponsored by the Chilean Communist Party at the University of Concepción in January 1960, to which he and Ferlighetti had been invited, following the publication of a Spanish translation of "Howl." Besides reading and talking about prosody and jazz, Ginsberg visited coal mines and saw the plight of workers:

> I live as if indifferent to the suffering of animals and men [he wrote] who die and groan to feed me and make my houses warm and bright—as if shielded from their sufferings, from knowledge and share of theirs by my tricky beard and wit. So that my poetry is all a half-celestial con, worth nothing to the bloodshot eyes of Physical sufferers in the mines and factories and fields. My original vow to help mankind in its sorry world-fate, on the boat to Columbia, is now being tested. Can I, as the Marxists claim [I do], remain aloof from the "final conflict" to bring bread and love to the masses? (Miles, 267)

Ginsberg did not have to struggle for the answer. It was no, he could not. And he did not. But it was on his terms as a visionary poet/prophet, not as a Marxist. Raising class-consciousness and striving for political change in his view were accomplished by expanding human consciousness. Revolutionary movements with purely materialist bases, he had seen throughout the 20th century, had devolved into reactionary tyrannies. In the 1960s his own social activity involved challenging the policies of some of those regimes as well as the policies of the U.S. Government. Expanded human consciousness, as Ginsberg understood it, was a consciousness of the interconnection of all being, of the seamless unity of life and death, of the awareness that reality was a precipitate of illusions. To stop the brutality and suffering that have historically defined reality, the illusory nature of reality has to be recognized and the freedom of individual consciousness must be cherished. His drug visions contributed to this belief.

Ginsberg found yage in Peru. After intense physical nausea and vomiting, he was overcome by visions of God, sensations of his own divinity, and despair at his own mortality. These experiences were then supplanted by an experience of loneliness and emptiness. He was disconsolate because he would die without children if he remained homosexual. Once again he experienced the attraction to his mother, which drove him to seek out states of mental disorientation, and once again he felt repulsed by her, and he feared consequently, by sexual relations with women generally. "Naomi dead in madhouse," he wrote,

My mother who I am to (be) return to in sex—all Mother the same—Birth—yet what was she, and what am I that I am her product and continue to live in the world of her madness? Is that my curse, which forbids me to live or die, to give birth, but be neither man nor woman … I resolved to bear babe, to bear Women, learn women—again…. They maybe are sent to save me, and I, not knowing in my pride, act Prophet over them and withdraw from their embrace and copulation and vomit of new birth. (Miles, 272)

FINDING HIMSELF LOST

Destruction was in the air internationally, but not the regeneration Ginsberg sought. The Cold War was in one of its most virulent phases, which would continue for several years, culminating in the Cuban missile crisis of October 1962. Apparent adversaries, the United States and the Soviet Union in their mutual pursuit of nuclear supremacy were partners in creating what at the time seemed inevitable: massive planetary death by nuclear annihilation. The presidential election of 1960 made awareness of the Cold War danger particularly strong as Kennedy and Nixon competed with each other to seem tougher in their stances with regard to the Soviet Union and China. The Cold War was not just evident in politics; it infused every aspect of American culture. Not only was Ginsberg unsteady in his self-identity and in relation to others, but he was alienated from the identity imposed upon him by American nationalism.

In March 1961, Ginsberg and Orlovsky left the United States for France, where Burroughs had been staying, but when Burroughs heard that Ginsberg and Orlovsky were arriving in Paris, he left for Tangiers. Alienated from human contact and from his own writing, Burroughs was doing "cut-ups," cutting out words from already written texts and piecing them together. It was a way of deconstructing and perhaps destroying identity. When Orlovsky and Ginsberg arrived in Tangiers, Burroughs was cold. It unnerved Ginsberg. At a time when he felt he did not know himself or Orlovsky, to find Burroughs not Burroughs, to find him also unknowable, was further destabilizing. Burroughs was applying the technique of cutting-up written

texts to human relationships, trying to get people to come to a
primary consciousness by taking apart their identities through a
merciless character-analysis. For Orlovsky it felt like a process
of cutting-down. Burroughs and his new lover taunted
Orlovsky, no match for Burroughs's intellect. Ginsberg, always
able to see the heavenly in the diabolical, later explained Burroughs's behavior to Orlovsky (and to himself) this way:

> I was confused and since I was clinging to my identity with
> you I could not see through your identity to your heart, and
> I think you wound up over-affirming your identity and
> pressing down harder on it while it was under attack, instead
> of just giving it up and coming out free. (Schumacher, 360)

Beside bearing Burroughs's attacks, Orlovsky was bearing
Ginsberg's conflict over his sexual identity and whether Ginsberg wanted him. Orlovsky was also facing his own
ambivalence about having a sexual relationship with Ginsberg
and whether he had not been "hypnotized" into sexual love
when he only experienced devotion, thus short-changing his
own apparently heterosexual disposition. Unable to bear Burroughs's attacks and Ginsberg's withdrawal and apparent
hostility, Orlovsky left Morocco for Greece. He said he wanted
time alone, and perhaps an end to what they both had considered their marriage.

Timothy Leary passed Orlovsky at customs as he was
leaving. Leary added to Ginsberg's anxiety by his skepticism
about the ability of poetry—as opposed to LSD—to unite
people in a common cosmic consciousness, challenging Ginsberg's role and identity as a poet. Typically, Ginsberg allowed
himself to realize

> that I was not tied down to being Allen Ginsberg—nor

being a poet—so [I] decided to let my identity drop and my awareness grew and went through a day of bliss as I found I was free—lots happened, I saw Bill and since my eyes had changed, he changed too and I saw that his cut-up meant also this cut up of identity, nothing worse really. (Schumacher, 360)

Corso, Ginsberg, Burroughs, and several others all took LSD with Leary. Whereas Corso delighted in the trip, Ginsberg was simply depressed by it, missing Orlovsky. Burroughs did not like the experience at all. (Schumacher, 359)

Ginsberg left Morocco at the end of August and sailed for Greece, where he spent his time traveling through the country and seeing the great artifacts of civilization but experiencing an empty grief over the conditions of the world and of his own soul. Of his relation to the conditions of the world he wrote his father, "I am getting plenty of 'Greek glory,' but it doesn't seem to stand up against the inhuman sense of things that is making my skin crawl lately." (Schumacher, 364) Of his spiritual condition he wrote in his notebook, "prodded on through the solitude bordered by olives and hills with the elevation of Hera's ruins on the right hand distance, singing to myself and the sky till tears came to my eyes while I lifted my voice, desolate in all that history, without any name for what I was." (Schumacher, 365)

Despite this crisis of identity and his sense of existential desolation, there still was a solid foundation upon which Ginsberg stood firmly: faith in a just society, where the bonds of identity—whether individual or national identity—did not crush humanity. Upon arriving in Greece, he received a commission from the magazine *Arriba* to write a poem about the Cuban revolution. Instead he wrote the essay, "Prose Contribution to Cuban Revolution." In it he approached the subjects that had been troubling him and laid out his politics and the bridge between spiritual psychology and politics:

> All governments including the Cuban are still operating within the rules of identity forced on them by already out-moded modes of consciousness. I say outmoded since it has brought all Govts. to edge of world destruction. No govt., not even the most Marxist revolutionary & well-intentioned like Cuba presumably, is guiltless in the general world mess, no one can afford to be righteous any more. Righteous & right & wrong are still fakes of the old suicidal identity. (Schumacher, 363–364)

After Greece, Ginsberg continued on to Israel. He hoped to meet Orlovsky and continue his confrontation with identity. Louis suggested in a letter,

> Perhaps in Israel you might feel some emotional reverbera-tions from the creation of that state…. We respond to some affinity with ancestral memories carried along in the blood stream and cached from ancient historical times in the genes…. Something in the psyche of the Jew was healed in the creation of the state of Israel. (Schumacher, 365)

But developing national identity was not what Ginsberg was striving for. "Jews and Arabs, Russians and Americans, all of them have preconceived notions about each other, not as people, but as objects of policy and prejudice," he told an inter-viewer from the *Jewish Post and Opinion*. To his father he wrote,

> [U]nless you have a pronounced single-minded dedication to an *exclusively Jewish* frame of mind in life, this place is not so exciting. Granted, it's fine as a refuge for the persecuted, and

granted also that the persecuted themselves are not so kindly to their own Arab minority.... It demands an *exclusively* Jewish mentality, whatever that is (everybody here's always arguing about that) and I found that a definite limitation on my own mentality which is Jewish enough but a lot more than that. This is XX Century and I still say the old order of Identity is a big nationalistic hang up on every side. (Schumacher, 366)

Individual identity and group nationalism were versions of the same destructive force for Ginsberg. Both signified attachment to one concept of being, one way of thinking, one way of feeling, and one way of seeing, whether individually or socially, which tried to preclude others. Since his Blake vision in Harlem in 1948, Ginsberg had been concerned with the obliteration of his own private identity through a transcendental consciousness. The tools for that transcendence were poetry, drugs, and psychotherapy. In his encounter with Burroughs in Tangiers, he had come close to a sense of lost selfhood and lost vocation; to an encounter with not being, which had been haunting him through his hallucinogenic visions and was often at the root of his poetry. It was, paradoxically, what Ginsberg believed to be the essential nonbeing of being that made being holy to him. It is also the continuing paradox of his life that the more Ginsberg challenged his identity, the more he devised and solidified his identity and image, and the more he became destabilized by the challenge, the closer he came to finding himself. He came into possession of himself when he seemed to be surrendering. Perhaps the reason lies in his fundamentally regarding himself as a heroic prophet: one who descends to the realms of death and returns bringing a vision of life. William Carlos Williams famously alludes to this power in Ginsberg in his introduction to "Howl."

The longest stop on Ginsberg's travels was in India, and it was the most important, for it served as both an end and a beginning. In India, Ginsberg found a culture that felt entirely congenial to him. In a letter to Kerouac he wrote:

Everybody in India is religious. It's weird, everybody ON to some saddhana (method), and has family guru or Brahmin priest and knows all about how the universe is a big illusion; it's totally unlike the West—it really is another dimension of time-history here…. It's assumed that all gods are unreal so one should respect all gods as purely subjective forms of meditation to fix the mind on one image and still it down and be peaceful—the gods are all interchangeable and friendly. (Schumacher, 370)

Ginsberg spent nearly 18 months living in and traveling through India, learning its culture, meeting its people, adjusting his vision of himself and the world according to its ways, and seeing an alternative to the Western reality that was tormenting him. "The subjective result on me of India," he wrote Kerouac,

has been to start dropping all spiritual activity initiated since Blake voice days and all mental activities I can discard, and stop straining at heaven's door and all that mysticism and drugs and cut-ups and gurus and fears of hell and desire for God and as such, as a result, in sum, I feel better and more relaxed. (Schumacher, 377)

When Ginsberg met the Dali Lama, the Dali Lama told him not to rely too heavily on LSD. When he asked Swami Shivananda where he could find a guru, Shivanada touched his heart and said, "The only guru is your own heart…. You'll know your guru when you see him because you'll love him; otherwise don't bother." (Schumacher, 372–373) Throughout India, Ginsberg visited opium dens, architectural and archeological wonders, heard Ravi Shankar play, gave poetry readings, watched holy festivals, bathed in the Ganges, meditated, and met holy men. One told him to take Blake as his guru. Another told him that poetry could be his yoga.

After the deconstructive power of yage and Burroughs's cut-ups, India was profoundly restorative for Ginsberg. In a *Paris Review* interview, some five years later, Ginsberg said that he had thought that God was death and that in order to "attain God" he had to break out of the body and die. "A whole series of India holy men pointed back to the body—getting in the body rather than getting out of the human form." (Schumacher, 377) He wrote Kerouac. "The ... feeling I got ... was always this kindly ... 'Don't worry, you're acceptable,' We love you,' 'Stop tormenting yourself'.... Get back in your skin,' ... 'accept your body'—which means 'accept your sexuality, accept your love, your loves; believe your own loves.' "

Back in the body, Ginsberg found his voice once again for poetry and for politics. It was the time of the Cuban missile crisis and of the escalation of the American presence in Vietnam. The violence and egotism of war and international standoffs reflected a different reality from the perception of love, dwelling in the body and the sacred continuum between life and death that had been reaffirmed for Ginsberg in India. (Schumacher, 387) But the destructive tendency of international Cold War politics acted paradoxically as a restorative. In the wake of possible nuclear annihilation, Ginsberg wrote Louis from India, "Is it worth doing anything about? Not that I don't like life and the human race but I wonder—*if* the race is threatened—if it is so important that the human experiment continues. I guess I would want it to be, yes." (Shumacher, 384)

The lesson of India was not to cling to anything, horrible or beautiful, but to accept death and to accept life. (Miles, 309) Ginsberg watched the burning of dead bodies in Calcutta on the steps leading down to the river within a circle of men who sat smoking marijuana and singing hymns (Miles, 310–11) and he learned not to be attached to life. But he and Orlovsky also found a man near death from starvation, covered in excrement, with flies swarming about his festering sores, eyes yellow with pus on the street near their rooms. With the aid of an orphan boy they paid, they took the man to the Ganges, bathed him, got him a doctor, fed him, and nursed him back to health. And they cared for several others similarly.

Toward the end of his stay in India, there was an incident that foreshadowed what several of the later trips Ginsberg took during the 1960s would be like. (Miles, 314ff.; Schumacher, 384ff.) After Ginsberg read some of his poems at the Benares Hindu University, the head of the English Department rose to condemn them for obscenity and vulgarity. Ginsberg retorted that the poetry was "not half as vulgar as the speech you're making now." The professor replied, "You have the nerve to make us … listen to that obscene 'poetry' and won't even listen to our criticisms?" The argument continued, with the professor's students joining in. "You wouldn't have talked to him that way if his skin was white," they shouted and accused Ginsberg of "corrupt[ing] our pure Hindi poetry." They sent a copy of *Howl* with the obscenities underlined to the CID, the Criminal Investigation Department of the local police. The CID was already investigating Ginsberg and Orlovsky, wondering what two Americans with little money were doing living among the people as they were. After two months they were ordered out of the country immediately, but finally an official in the Home Ministry bureaucracy understood that they were "here on an intellectual level," and extended their visas for six months. In response to the exchange at the Hindu University, Ginsberg imposed upon himself the discipline of tempering his anger and belligerence. He saw them as signs of his attachment to his own ego and became aware that such self-assertion made each side stiffen with resistance and righteousness, as his response had. (Schumacher, 387) It was an insight that would stay with him as he became more and more a public man.

When Ginsberg left India for Vancouver, British Columbia, to participate in a poetry seminar that the poet Robert Creeley had organized there, Orlovsky remained in India. Their relationship had deteriorated. They were hardly speaking and Orlovsky was shooting morphine and bitterly telling Ginsberg that he was washed up as a poet, had nothing to say, and was being untrue to himself by taking money for his readings or participating in the conference.

On the way to Vancouver, Ginsberg stopped in Vietnam where he spoke with American reporters who told him of the horrors of the war that had already begun to occur, but he demurred out of fear when offered to go firsthand into the countryside to see the war. He stopped in Cambodia, too, and spent five days exploring the ruins of the 12th-century temple at Angkor Wat. His journey culminated in a visit to Japan, where he experienced a remarkable return to a condition of peacefulness that had entirely eroded by the time he left Burroughs in Tangiers:

> I suddenly didn't want to be *dominated* by that nonhuman any more, or even be dominated by the moral obligation to enlarge my consciousness any more, or do anything any more except *be* my heart—which just desired to be and be alive now.... I was suddenly free to love myself again, and therefore love the people around me, in the form that they already were. And love myself in my own form as I am. I

started weeping and sobbing that I was still alive in a body that was going to die. Then I began looking around on the train and seeing all the other mortal faces … and I saw how exquisitely dear they all were—we all were—so I pulled out my notebook, while the illumination was still glowing in my body, and, while my breath was still fitted to weeping, scribbled everything that came into my thought-stream. Schumacher, 393–4)

1963–1965: BECOMING AN ACTIVIST

Ginsberg returned to San Francisco at the end of July 1963, after three weeks at the Vancouver poetry conference—which was as much an exploration of sensual liberty among teachers and students as it was of poetry—and reconnected with many old friends including Michael McClure, Ferlinghetti, Neal Cassady (recently released from San Quentin), and Lucien Carr, who had just happened to come out from New York on a lark. Ginsberg had mellowed. His politics showed it, too. In San Francisco his active involvement in the anti-Vietnam War movement began when he picketed the appearance of Madame Nhu at the Sheraton Palace Hotel. Madame Nhu, wife of Vietnam's chief of secret police and the sister-in-law of Ngo Dinh Diem, the U.S.-installed dictator of South Vietnam, was visiting San Francisco as part of a public relations tour sponsored by the U.S. State Department. Ginsberg joined hundreds of demonstrators to picket her talk. On the picket line, he carried a sign bearing a short poem against war itself, but not vilifying Madame Nhu. He told reporters, "'I'm here in the picket line trying to be tender to Madame Nhu and Mao Tsetung. Or better, asking them to be tender." His philosophy of opposition was framed by his conviction that "Anger and fury of left wing will only drive the humanoid bureaucrats and cops into deeper humanoidism. Be kind to cops; they're not cops, they're people in disguise who've been deceived by their own disguise." (Miles, 331) It is not a very different insight from the one he had in the Columbia bookstore after his Blake vision in 1948, when he saw every face masked against the expression of true humanity. The same day that Ginsberg introduced "Flower Power," to the demonstration against Madame Nhu, he achieved the iconic stature he would carry for the rest of his life when he appeared in *L'il Abner*, a hugely popular newspaper comic strip. Al Capp, a staunch supporter of the Vietnam War, lampooned him as the "Hairy-Breasted Ginsbird." (Schumacher, 400)

A few weeks later, demonstrating Ginsberg's even-handed opposition to both camps in the Cold War, and his concern for freedom independent of the arguments of nationalism or ideology, he confronted Tamara Motoyleva, a Soviet specialist in American literature on a Soviet-sponsored visit to the United States, regarding censorship in Soviet-controlled countries. She simultaneously defended it and denied it existed. Ginsberg's balanced dedication to humanity over abstraction or ideology was a harbinger of his positions in Cuba and Czechoslovakia a few years later.

At the end of November, a week after John Kennedy's assassination, Ginsberg returned to Manhattan. He and Orlovsky had been writing to each other and tenderness had returned to their relationship:

I always feel bad to part from you if we're cold to each other, and I feel happy to be alone when I know there's still a little tender look between us left in eternity. For no matter what happens, I always want to love you. (Miles, 321)

They took an apartment on the Lower East Side, and as usual it became a haven for many, including Orlovsky's brother Julius, whom they took out of a mental institution after a dozen years' confinement. Kerouac, whose mother had become an even more controlling force in his life, was unavailable. Gregory Corso, who was now married and a father, had cracked up and been hospitalized for a brief period. Marretta Greer, a waif of a girl who was returning from India, knocked at Ginsberg's door seeking a place to stay. They became lovers for years to come when she was not in India.

Ginsberg spent two years in New York immersing himself in the culture of the Lower East Side. He was interested in New York's underground film scene and spent time at Andy Warhol's Factory and appeared in a short Warhol film sitting on a couch. Jonas Mekas, who ran the Film-Makers Cooperative, introduced him to Barbara Rubin, who made lyrical cinema constructions by layering several strips of film, all spontaneously shot, on top of each other. She and Ginsberg became lovers but parted when he refused to follow her in her spiritual conversion to Hassidic Judaism. His long friendship with Bob Dylan began, too, when Al Aronowitz, who in 1957 had written *The New York Post* series on the Beats, introduced them. Ginsberg also spent time with the people in the Kerista collective, a Lower East Side commune whose members practiced collective ownership of resources and free love.

Ginsberg's involvement in the scene was not just cultural. Ginsberg lobbied in New York City to prevent coffee houses from being barred from presenting poetry readings; he was active in the defense of comedian Lenny Bruce, who was being prosecuted for his nightclub act; and he testified in defense of Jonas Mekas, who was being prosecuted for screening Jack Smith's underground movie *Flaming Creatures* and Jean Genet's film, *Chant d'Amour*. He testified at the obscenity trial for *Naked Lunch* in Boston; he joined with Ed Sanders, a poet and singer in the rock group *The Fugs,* in starting Lemar, an organization dedicated to the legalization of marijuana; and he picketed the Women's House of Detention in Greenwich Village, calling for the release of women imprisoned for drug use.

chapter

seven

King of the May

*… the Marxists have beat me upon the street,
kept me up all night in Police Station, followed me thru
Springtime …*

—Allen Ginsberg, "Kral Majales"

CUBA

In January 1965, Ginsberg traveled to Cuba as the guest of the Cuban government to participate in an arts conference. Six years earlier, Fidel Castro and Che Guevara and a force of guerillas had defeated the army of Fulgencio Batista, the Cuban dictator, established a revolutionary government, and begun economic and social reforms. In August 1960, Castro nationalized foreign-owned property. The United States Government retaliated by imposing a trade embargo on Cuba, isolating Cuba and, by forcing it to depend on the Soviet Union for trade and aid, put it in the Soviet bloc in the Cold War. By the time Ginsberg arrived in Cuba, much had been accomplished economically and socially to alleviate hunger, malnutrition, illiteracy, and poor medical care. For that, Ginsberg supported the revolution, "people working and building, like they say, a new society—which is remarkable for any South American country." And he believed that the Cubans "obviously do have a tough struggle to survive[;] their defiance and resentment of U.S. obnoxious intrusion and blockade is understandable completely." (Schumacher, 426–427)

But he also was not going to conform to or accept ideological dicta and police state practices in Cuba, even if they were consequences of an American threat—which the failed CIA invasion at the Bay of Pigs in 1962 showed to be a reasonable Cuban fear—any more than he would in the United States. In Cuba, therefore, Ginsberg met with young poets who approached him and told him that although they supported the revolution, it was being betrayed because of the existence of *Lacra Social,* a special branch of the police, and that writers, homosexuals, and beatniks were being arrested. In fact, several of those with whom Ginsberg met were detained during his stay after seeing him. Ginsberg had already been vocal against the Cuban laws criminalizing marijuana use when he questioned a Cuban delegation in New York City in 1960. Now in interviews with Cuban journalists and conversations with government officials, he brought up the issues of capital punishment, homosexuality, literary censorship, suppression of speech, and marijuana use.

With regard to the persecution of homosexuals, Haydee Santamaria, the Minister of Culture, told Ginsberg that homosexuals "were making public spectacles of themselves and seducing impressionable young boys." (Schumacher, 425) About marijuana, she said with unarguable finality, "It has always been a crime and it's definitely a crime and that's how it must be for the time being. That's the policy we've adopted." As for free speech and democratic argument: "Though you may discuss such ideas" [sexual freedom and legalizing marijuana] "with people on a high level or mature officials ... we cannot have you spreading such ideas which are against the laws of our country and our policy among our young people." (Schumacher, 426) Regarding marijuana and homosexuality, then, the Cuban Government and the United States Government were in agreement. But just as he spoke his mind publicly in the United States, so, too, he did in Cuba. For Ginsberg, the liberty of the individual and the quest to discover the mysteries of consciousness trumped the order of the State, even a nominally revolutionary Marxist State.

At 8:00 one morning, before his stay in Cuba was scheduled to end, Ginsberg was taken from his hotel by a government official and three soldiers, held in a small cell with only a chair, given cigarettes and newspapers, and then driven to the airport and put on a plane to Prague, the only route between Cuba and the United States because of the United States embargo. Ginsberg concluded from his experience in Cuba "that the more the United States put pressure on Cuba, the more power the right wing military, police bureaucracy and Party hacks would get.

The real problem was to relieve the pressure in America, to end the blockade rather than to 'blame' the Cuban Revolution, Castro, or Marxism." (Schumacher, 429) It was characteristic of Ginsberg to try to solve a problem not by aggression but by undoing its cause. He was not excusing or accepting Cuban injustices. He was trying to look at the cause of the problem rather than the symptoms by which it expressed itself. It was also his style to bring issues to a head. "In Cuba, I committed about every 'infraction of totalitarian laws' I could think of, verbally, and they finally flipped out and gave me the bum's rush," he told his father. (Schumacher, 429)

CZECHOSLOVAKIA

Perhaps Ginsberg had been naïve regarding Cuba, had believed that there was a spirit to the revolution that would enable his humanist cries for the freedom of the soul's complexity to be heard. He knew better with regard to Czechoslovakia and tried to be careful. The country was governed by an entrenched and brutal government bureaucracy controlled by the Soviet Union, and it ruled with an iron fist. At the time that Ginsberg visited, however, a thaw was beginning, and the Prague Spring would be in full bloom three years later before being crushed by Soviet tanks. There was a coffee house in Prague where young people hung out and where poetry was read, the *Viola Café*. Ginsberg was known already and had a following. "Howl" and other poems had been translated into Czech. Homosexuality, moreover, was not a crime in Czechoslovakia as it was in Cuba. He read his poetry, lectured on Henry Miller, and discussed homosexuality and LSD. He was a "guest of the State," and of the Writer's Union, and was put up in a large suite in a hotel and given $75 spending money.

Ginsberg left Czechoslovakia for two weeks to visit Russia where some of his mother's family lived, and he did find his mother's cousin, Joe Levy, and spent time with him looking at old photographs and discussing family history. Shepherded through his visit to Russia by an escort from the Writer's Union, however, Ginsberg was coached in how to behave and what was expected of him. Very diplomatically he was told it was better not to mention jailed Russian poet Joseph Brodsky and that people in the Soviet Union had "normal" sexual relations and just would not be interested in homosexuality or reading Henry Miller. He met with the world-renowned Russian poet Yevgeny Yevtushenko, who was very friendly, but refused to talk about homosexuality or LSD, calling them Ginsberg's personal problems. But Yevtushenko did admit that he had a number of good poems that could not be published in the Soviet Union and that among his published poems many alterations had been made to satisfy the censors. Ginsberg visited the Kremlin and the Hermitage museum in Leningrad, attended concerts and the ballet, and met with professors, translators, and students—for whom he read from his poetry and answered questions about Kerouac and spontaneous composition. Returning to Prague by way of Poland, Ginsberg stopped to see the scant remaining traces of the Warsaw Ghetto, where Jews had unsuccessfully resisted Nazis troops, and visited the Nazi death camp at Auschwitz.

He returned to Prague just in time for May Day. Rather than the dour celebration of military might and discipline, as it was in the Soviet Union, the Czech authorities were allowing the traditional, medieval May Day festival that had been forbidden since they had seized power after World War II. Ginsberg was asked by his friend, the Czech poet Josef Skvorecky, to be King of the May. He accepted and was elected and driven through the streets by a crowd of a hundred thousand festive young people. The bacchanalia did not sit well with the authorities in the Czech Communist Party and Ginsberg was dethroned. But his troubles in Czechoslovakia were only beginning.

Two days after the May Day celebration, Ginsberg discovered a notebook was missing from his room. That night, upon leaving a bar where two strangers in business suits had been buying him drinks, he was stopped by the police. Because he did not have his passport on him, he was taken to the police station, questioned, and released. Two nights later, as Ginsberg was walking in Prague with two friends an assailant screamed "fairy" in Czech at Ginsberg, knocked him down, pursued him when Ginsberg got up and fled, and assaulted him again. The police arrived, brandishing clubs, and took them all to the stationhouse, where Ginsberg's assailant accused Ginsberg of exposing himself and charged that Ginsberg and his two companions had tried to assault him. When Ginsberg demanded to see an official from the American embassy, the police released everyone including the assailant, making Ginsberg believe the whole thing was a setup.

The next morning Ginsberg bought a ticket for London and then did a radio interview. Afterwards he was sitting in a restaurant with friends when plainclothes police approached and told him to come with them, they had his notebook. At the police station, he was told the notebook was being turned over to the public prosecutor to see if it contained any "illegal writings." (Schumacher, 442) The next morning, during breakfast at a café, Ginsberg was again taken into custody. At the police station he was told that because he was a bad and corrupting influence on Czechoslovakian youth, he was being put on the next flight to London. He was driven to his hotel, put under guard until the time of his flight and then taken to the airport.

When he arrived in London, Ginsberg got in touch with Bob Dylan who was there on tour, making the documentary *Don't Look Back*. Dylan invited Ginsberg to attend his concerts and introduced him to the Beatles. After traveling around England and giving a reading in Liverpool, Ginsberg organized the International Poetry reading at the Royal Albert Hall. Before returning to the United States, he spent a week in Paris.

Back in the United States, Ginsberg spent hardly more than a week in New York before he and Orlovsky went out to California for a poetry conference at Berkeley. With the money he received from a Guggenheim grant he was awarded in 1965, Ginsberg bought a Volkswagen bus. He put a bed, a refrigerator, and a desk in it. Bob Dylan had given him $600 to buy a reel-to-reel tape recorder, and he traveled through the United States, observing the scene and orally composing poetry, including the "Wichita Vortex Sutra."

ACTIVIST POET

Ginsberg's experiences in Cuba and Czechoslovakia established him as an activist poet whose exploration of consciousness was not only a literary exercise or an attempt to know himself but a criticism of life and a dedication to improving the conditions of life. Ginsberg was convinced that Shelley's description of poets as unacknowledged legislators was accurate. By the mid-1960s, Ginsberg had moved from being a catalytic commentator on American life to a social, political, and even spiritual force who seemed to have a personal relationship with history. As he attempted to direct the course of events, the course of his life and the course of American politics converged. Just as his very way of being, as well as his speech and his activity, had brought the wrath of the governments of Cuba and Czechoslovakia upon him, so too, in the United States, there were elements of the government intent upon discrediting him. When Ginsberg arrived in New York, he was strip-searched at the airport. The F.B.I. had reopened a dossier on him and Orlovsky, concerned that they were involved in narcotics smuggling. Ginsberg's file

described him as "disruptive and possibly violent." (Schumacher, 448)

But it was neither violence nor disruption that Ginsberg was
cultivating. Through poetry, he was trying to attain cosmic
connection and human harmony. America was making him
want to be a magician as well as a saint. (Schumacher, 449) As a
poet, Ginsberg wrought influence through words. As a magician, he hoped to influence the course of events by the very
vibration of his being, not only by his words, but by the fre-
quencies of his breath and the timbre of his voice. In testimony
before the United States Senate Judiciary Subcommittee on
Juvenile Delinquency regarding his experiences with LSD,
Ginsberg revealed more about the Gandhian nature of his political commitment than about the drug: "The day I took the
LSD was the same day that President Johnson went into the
operating room for his gall bladder illness," Ginsberg testified:

> As I walked in the forest, wondering what my feelings
> toward him were ... the awesome place I was in impressed
> me with its old tree and ocean cliff majesty. Many tiny jew-
> eled violet flowers along the path of a living brook ... huge
> Pacific watery shore. I saw a friend [Peter Orlovsky] dancing
> long haired before giant green waves, under cliffs ... and a
> great yellow sun veiled with mist hanging over the planet's
> ocean horizon. Armies at war on the other side of the planet.
> Berkeley's Vietnam protestors sadly preparing manifestos for
> our march toward Oakland police and Hell's Angels, and the
> President...himself experiencing what fear or grief? I realized
> that more vile words from me would send out negative
> vibrations into the atmosphere—more hatred amassed
> against his poor flesh and soul on trial. So I knelt on the
> sand surrounded by masses of green kelp washed up by a
> storm, and prayed for President Johnson's tranquil health.

Certainly more public hostility would not help him or me or anyone come through to some less rigid and more flexible awareness of ourselves as Victim. (Schumacher, 451)

Contrasting the Edenic pastoral with the violent realities of the political situation, Ginsberg recalled the Vietnam War and also "Berkeley's Vietnam protestors sadly preparing manifestos for our march toward Oakland police and Hell's Angels." The Hell's Angels motorcycle gang, their patriotism offended, had disrupted an antiwar demonstration in Berkeley as police looked on. The Angels announced they would attack the next planned demonstration, too, and the organizers of the Vietnam Day Committee were searching for a response. One recurring idea was that the demonstrators ought to come prepared to fight back. Seeking to find common ground upon which the antiwar demonstrators and the Hell's Angels might meet, Ginsberg argued against such tactics—which would only add violence to violence and contradict the purpose of the march— and in the he process redefined the nature of political demonstration:

> It wasn't just a political march where people were supposed to run and march angry, shouting slogans. It could be seen as theater.... And given the situation, the best kind of theater would manifest the Peace that we were protesting. Pro-test being 'pro-attestation,' testimony in favor of something. So if we were going to be a peace-protest march, then we should have to be peaceful, and being peaceful took skillful means under such anxious circumstances. (Schumacher, 453)

Ginsberg laid out some of the means to make "an unmistakable statement OUTSIDE the war psychology which is leading nowhere." In "How to Make a March/Spectacle," he suggested the peace parade incorporate floats, flowers, music, papier-mâché puppets, costumes, mimes, and pennants. "The parade can embody an example of peaceable health which is the reverse of fighting back blindly." (Schumacher, 453)

The Hell's Angels were not impressed, and still promised to attack. Hoping for better communication, Ginsberg organized an open forum at San Jose State College for an informal debate between the organizers of the Vietnam Day Committee and the Hell's Angels. But that, too, failed. The Angels insisted that the demonstrators were communists who had to be stopped, even if bloodied, and the audience cheered them on.

As a last measure, Ginsberg arranged a private meeting with the bikers. Ginsberg, parade organizers, Ken Kesey, and a band of costumed Merry Pranksters met a group of Hell's Angels at the home of Sonny Barger, president of the Oakland chapter of the Hell's Angels. Ginsberg brought LSD, and everyone dropped acid but him. He was afraid the tension of the situation would lead to a bad trip for him. Despite the acid, negotiations went badly; the Hell's Angels, in the name of patriotism, were spoiling for a fight. Picking up his harmonium, Ginsberg began to chant the Prajnaparamita Sutra: "simply a tone of voice from the abdomen," a "monosyllabic deep-voiced monochordal chant." The magic worked. Soon everyone was chanting. "It brought the whole scene,' Ginsberg later observed,

> down from the argument to some kind of common tone— because they were desperate too…. They didn't know what else to do except argue and maintain their righteous wrath. It settled everybody's breath there in a neutral territory where there was neither attack nor defense." (Schumacher, 455)

A few days later, the Hell's Angels announced in a letter to the

San Francisco Examiner that they would not demean themselves by confronting the demonstrators, but had sent a telegram to President Johnson offering to fight the Communists in South Vietnam. Johnson did not respond, but the march proceeded peacefully, and soon after, Kesey threw a big party for beatniks, hippies, Pranksters, peace protestors, and Hell's Angels.

Ginsberg's success with the Hell's Angels defined the times. For another year, antiwar activity was marked by an optimistic faith that gentleness could overcome brutality and that creating harmony was the way to end discord. It was a time of flowers and chanting and asserting spiritual unity. Ginsberg became the very embodiment of the spirit of the times. He was one of the principal organizers of the Human Be-In in San Francisco's Golden Gate Park in January 1967. A massive gathering of people dedicated to the sensual expression of spirituality, the Human Be-In brought together antiwar activists; advocates of consciousness expansion through pharmacology, poetry, and meditation; rock bands like the Grateful Dead and the Jefferson Airplane—what Theodore Rozack would soon call the counter-culture. Following the Be-In, Ginsberg spent the winter touring the United States, giving poetry readings, and discussing the social and political situation at universities and public forums.

In the summer of 1967, Ginsberg returned to Europe. Early in July he read at the Spoleto Festival in Italy (and was taken into custody briefly by the Italian police for language in his poetry that they considered objectionable). He met his father and Edith on their first visit to Europe, too, and showed them around. He also spent several days with another father figure, Ezra Pound.

It is easy to see Ginsberg taking William Carlos Williams for a model. He was on the side of the angels. But Ezra Pound was not. Believing that Mussolini was the Thomas Jefferson of Italy and that Jews were responsible for the demonized economics of

Straight Culture/Beat Culture

For Ginsberg, the interview was almost an art form in itself. He gave interviews freely and spoke candidly. In the following excerpt he spoke of the perceived Beatnik threat to American culture in the 1950s:

AG: In 1959, when LIFE [November 30] magazine came around I said, 'If they think that we got something going, they must be scraping the bottom of their own barrel and they must be in a pretty deprived place [laughter].' Actually, after I talked to [LIFE writer, Paul O'Neil], I lay in bed trembling, realizing that we had an enormous responsibility. If the mainstream culture was so vulnerable...then they must be pretty empty like a paper tiger, and we would have to supply some kind of real culture in America, or real inspiration. That was back in '59. So from then on there was what Pat Buchanan now calls a spiritual war for the soul of America. And in '59 I did write an essay saying exactly that. By 1962 or '63, Cardinal Francis Spellman and J. Edgar Hoover were denouncing the Beatniks along with the eggheads, communists, and others as the greatest threats to America.

Seth Goddard: Did you take any pride in being considered such a threat to America?

AG: No. It was a dismay that they were so mean-spirited and lacking in humor and enthusiasm [for] old American values. What would they do with Walt Whitman? What would they do with Thoreau if they were going to do that with us? They were out of sync with basic American values—Emerson, Thoreau, and all that.... There was that old Americanist tradition of recognition of the land and the people and the gawky awkward beauty of the individual eccentric citizen.

(*www.life.com/Life/boomers/ginsberg.html*)

usury, what Pound called *Usura*, he supported the fascists in the Second World War and made propaganda radio broadcasts for Mussolini. After the war, American forces took Pound prisoner and ultimately he was confined as a madman in Saint Elizabeth's hospital in Washington D.C. for 12 years rather than tried as a traitor.

When Ginsberg met him, Pound had been living in Italy since his release from Saint Elizabeth's. He was leaving the *Cantos*, his ongoing epic, unfinished, and he hardly spoke. But in a terse conversation with Ginsberg about himself and his poetry, he said perhaps all that needed to be said when he told Ginsberg that during his lifetime he had been preoccupied "with irrelevant and stupid things." He added "The worst mistake I made was the stupid, suburban prejudice of antisemitism. All along, that spoiled everything." It was something he had never said publicly before. "It's lovely to hear you say that," Ginsberg replied, and tried to soothe him by observing that in his poetry, nevertheless, Pound showed the map of a mind as it thought, and brought the duration of the breath to be the measure of poetry, profoundly thereby influencing succeeding generations of poets. Pound remained withdrawn and spiritually depressed, but parting he inscribed a volume of his *Cantos* to Ginsberg and at Ginsberg's request Pound gave him his blessing, "for whatever it's worth." (Schumacher, 490–495)

Ginsberg spent time in England that summer, too, before returning to Italy for his visit with Pound. He spoke at the conference convened by R.D. Laing, and Gregory Bateson on "The Dialectics of Liberation," he sat in on a recording session when John Lennon and Paul McCartney joined Keith Richards and Mick Jagger in the chorus of "We Love You," about the drug busts of both the Stones, and he traveled through the British Isles, taking LSD and writing poetry, including "Wales Visitation," which appeared in the volume *Planet News* that Ferlinghetti published the following year.

While Ginsberg was visiting Pound, multitudes of people in the United States who were opposed to the War in Vietnam converged on the Pentagon in Washington to demand the war's end. Although he was in Italy and not Washington, D.C. at the time of the march, Ginsberg had been one of the principal architects of its major rite. Conceiving of a demonstration as theater, Ginsberg created the scenario "Exorcising the Pentagon" along with Lower East Side poets and members of *The Fugs* Ed Sanders and Tuli Kupferberg. There was a magic circle formed around the Pentagon by a group of shamanist/poets who chanted words Ginsberg wrote for the occasion. If the Pentagon had levitated, the ritual would have been successful, evil spirits exorcised, and everybody could go home. But since it did not, it became the task of the demonstrators to "exorcise" the Pentagon themselves by surrounding it and sitting in nonviolently until the war was stopped.

Thousands did sit on the blacktop surrounding the five-sided building, whose porches were manned by platoons of soldiers pointing loaded guns at the crowd. By morning, with beatings and arrests and some antiwar protestors leaving on their own throughout the night—rather than be among the next wave rifle-butted and arrested—the demonstrators had been cleared from the areas immediately surrounding the Pentagon. The mood was not defeatist, however. There were stories, which turned out to be true, that several of the soldiers had responded to the steady chanting of "Join us! Join us!" by putting down their rifles and doing so.

In New York City on December 5, Ginsberg was arrested when he participated in Stop the Draft Week demonstrations during which thousands of protestors mobilized in Battery Park and then spread out in groups throughout lower Manhattan, trying to block access to the Army's Whitehall Street Induction Center. It was herald to the kind of confrontations between demonstrators and police that would mark 1968. The floral beneficence that had sweetened the nature of opposition in 1967 had faded, and the stench of the Vietnam War was causing irritation.

The fear that American democracy had entirely broken down followed upon a series of events early in 1968. On January 5, Dr. Benjamin Spock and four others were indicted on federal charges of conspiring to counsel draft evasion. On February 8, three black students were killed and 27 wounded in Orangeburg, South Carolina, when state troopers fired at demonstrators demanding the integration of the local bowling alley. On April 4, the Reverend Dr. Martin Luther King, Jr. was assassinated. Riots in the black sections of 100 American cities followed, for King's death suggested that the possibility of an end to American racism through nonviolent struggle was chimerical. Voices calling for confrontation, violence, and revenge, like Eldridge Cleaver's, Rap Brown's, or Ron Karenga's were in the ascendancy. On April 23, the students of Columbia University in New York took over the administrative offices and several academic buildings in response to the university's ties to the U.S. Institute for Defense Analysis and the university's plan to build a gymnasium in Morningside Park, taking land away from the neighboring black community in Harlem. The students were brutally ejected by the police. On April 27, in Chicago, at the end of an antiwar march, the police drove into the crowd of dispersing demonstrators, swinging clubs. On June 5, Robert Kennedy, senator from New York, brother of the slain president, a candidate for the Democratic Party's presidential nomination, and, for many of those who opposed the war, the embodiment of their hope, was assassinated. On June 14, Dr. Spock and four other defendants were convicted of counseling draft resistance. In Europe too, repression and resistance were evident in the student/worker uprisings in France in May and in Czechoslovakia in August, when Soviet tanks rolled into Prague.

Inside the climate created by these events, thousands of antiwar demonstrators converged on Chicago to assert their opposition to the war during the Democratic National Convention. Ginsberg had been in on the planning from the beginning when Abbie Hoffman, one of the demonstration's main organizers, asked him to be a cosponsor and laid out a scenario very much resembling the kind Ginsberg had devised for affirmative demonstrations in Berkeley. But Chicago's Mayor Richard J. Daley, an old-line Democrat and a quintessential machine politician, refused to issue permits. It was impossible to call the demonstration off, for the outraged would come to Chicago no matter what, and Ginsberg decided it was his responsibility to be there to try to calm a situation he feared would be explosive. By refusing to issue permits for the antiwar events planned during the Democratic Convention, Mayor Daley—who had shown the quality of his character when he ordered police to "shoot to kill" during an upheaval in the black community in Chicago following Martin King's assassination—transformed what might have been another Be-In *cum* Teach-In into a brutal confrontation between thousands of demonstrators, convention delegates, and hapless bystanders with a police force on the rampage, as the Walker Commission report determined it was. (*www.geocities.com/Athens/Delphi/1553/ricsumm.html*)

Ginsberg stayed in Lincoln Park every night chanting, sometimes for as long as seven hours straight, trying to keep crowds of mostly young people calm as the police rioted around them. Unlike with the Hell's Angels, chanting did not pacify the police, and groups of chanters as well as marchers were attacked. Nevertheless, the experience of chanting over long periods of time—"I began to feel a funny tingling in my feet that spread until my whole body was one rigid electrical tingling—a solid mass of lights."—even if it did not serve as protection from the police, made Ginsberg

> realize that it was possible through chanting to make advances on the body and literally to alter states of consciousness. I'd got to euphorias, ecstasies of pleasure, years before; but this was the first time I'd gotten neurological body sensations, cellular extensions of some kind of cosmic consciousness within my body. (Miles, 417)

Following the rout in Chicago, there were a great many who withdrew from city life and confrontational political activity, just as some, like the Weathermen, dedicated themselves to "revolutionary" violence. Like many antiwar movement people who had actively engaged in working for peace, civil rights, and social change, Ginsberg returned to the "land." He had bought a farm in July 1968 in Cherry Valley, New York, not only as a retreat from political chaos, but as a refuge for Orlovsky, who had succumbed to the strain of living on New York's Lower East Side inside the web of Ginsberg's career and suffered periods of mental derangement and drug addiction.

Their life together was complicated. Although they saw their relationship as a marriage and had vowed a life-long commitment to each other, which they maintained, that commitment did not preclude having other lovers and other relationships. This was especially important for Orlovsky who felt himself to be essentially heterosexual and whose sexual relations with Ginsberg seems to have been the result not of desire for Ginsberg but of desire to please Ginsberg. But such an attitude took its toll, and periodically Orlovsky refused to have sexual relations with Ginsberg. At a time of such a tension in their relationship, Ginsberg wrote him:

> I'm happy making it with you alone as long as we make it. I just chase after boys as a substitute when I get the idea that you don't want to be stuck with me and that I'm generally too old and repulsive to you now after so much famil-iarity.... I really got the idea ... that you basically don't dig making it with me, and so as not to lay my needs on you, I diverted lovemaking to others and accepted the situation cheerfully rather than getting hung up on it and laying guilt on you or me.... If you've been at all avoiding love-making with me because you think I need or deserve younger various cats, well stop that thought and let's make it more again. I'd rather stick with you, if it were still pleasant to you.... I have need for love touch and sex come but I'm not so nuts as to think that you or anybody has to find me sexy—so I've just been taking what comes to me, without my having to force the situation by willpower. (Miles, 399–400)

But Orlovsky's ambivalence toward homosexuality and his relationships with women, and Ginsberg's numerous sexual relationships with males and females, constituted only part of the difficulty of their relationship. Ginsberg's worldwide celebrity and his involvement in fashioning the persona Allen Ginsberg, at work even when he was trying to transcend that identity, put him and Orlovsky in very different worlds. He left Orlovsky alone frequently, and even when Orlovsky was with him, he was very much in Ginsberg's shadow. Inevitably, their relationship came to mirror Ginsberg's parents' marriage. Like Naomi, Orlovsky was a tormented soul, sometimes violent, at times delusional—imagining the house on fire, thinking that the moldings were bugged—periodically in and out of mental hospitals. And Ginsberg, like his father, bore the burden of his partner's madness and his own responsibilities.

The farm was supposed to be a haven, and for a time Orlovsky was off drugs and involved in the healthy demanding work of fixing buildings, tending the land, and preparing for winter. But the farm was a communal enterprise, as all Ginsberg's living arrangements were, and visitors like Gregory Corso and Herbert Huncke who came to stay brought alcohol and drugs with them, and Orlovsky often succumbed. He even sold Ginsberg's letters to him to buy drugs, which he hid all over the farm.

Despite periods of rancor and conflict, and despite an automobile accident that put him in a cast, Ginsberg was continuing his work at the farm. He had become more involved with chanting and with composing music. In October 1971, Bob Dylan and the composer David Amram—who set "Pull My Daisy" to music—went to hear Ginsberg and Orlovsky do a joint reading at New York Univesity's Loeb Student Center. After the reading they went back to Ginsberg's apartment and improvised songs together, Dylan showing Ginsberg how to play some new chord changes and 12-bar blues on the harmonium. A week or so later, Dylan took Ginsberg to a recording studio and they laid down some tracks that were released in the early 1980s. A few days before that session, Ginsberg had sung mantras and some of his settings of Blake poems with John Lennon, Klaus Voorman, Ringo Starr, and Phil Specter backing him up during a release party for Lennon's album, *Imagine*. At the farm, Ginsberg continued to work on musical settings for Blake's *Songs of Innocence* and *Songs of Experience*, hoping to create the feel of Blake's own performances of the poems and to reproduce in the music Blake's own voice, a voice he had seriously identified with since his audio-vision of Blake in 1948 in Harlem.

An Uncarved Block

O give me ground for next a step
To stagger walking in my sleep.
—Paul Goodman, *The Empire City*

SPIRITUAL OBEDIENCE

It would be simplistic to say that Ginsberg formed friendships in order to gather matter for literature, and it would, additionally, be unfair, but it is nevertheless true that for Ginsberg, life and art were inseparable. Just as he used his experience of the world around him in his verse, his poetry being the vehicle for organizing his perception, so every significant relationship significantly influenced the matter and the manner of his work. Joining Burroughs, Cassady (who had died in 1968), Kerouac (who had died in 1969), Williams, and Pound as figures whose influence profoundly directed the course of Ginsberg's work and his life was the Tibetan Lama Chogyam Trungpa, Rinpoche, whom Ginsberg first met—quite accidentally—during the summer of 1970.

Ginsberg was walking with Louis in New York City when Louis felt overcome by the heat. Ginsberg asked two men for whom a taxi had stopped if he could "steal" their cab, explaining his father was not well. One of the men was Trungpa, believed to be the reincarnation of the tenth Trungpa Tulku, supreme abbot of the Surmang group of monasteries in the region of Tsighai, China, where he was born and a practitioner of "Wild Wisdom," a radical Buddhism that sought to break the hold of attachment by creating confrontations that put disciples entirely at odds with themselves. The other man, his assistant, recognized Allen Ginsberg, and they exchanged addresses.

In the spring of 1971, Ginsberg was in Berkeley to oversee the compilation of his recorded readings onto a master tape. Trungpa happened to be there, too, to deliver a speech. Ginsberg visited him at his hotel before the talk and, immediately, the nature of their relationship was established. As he had with Kerouac, Cassady—and Orlovsky, too, but Orlovsky was not the dominating figure the other two were—Ginsberg fell in love with Trungpa, and that meant he gave himself to him, feeling himself mastered by him. Trungpa became Ginsberg's spiritual guru and Ginsberg became his poetry guru, helping with the translation of his poetry and, later, writing the introduction to a volume of his poems. Trungpa's effect on Ginsberg's poetry was just as immediate as his effect on his physiognomy.

From the beginning of his career in 1956, Ginsberg existed publicly as more than a celebrity; he was an icon, first of the

Files on Ginsberg

After being searched at the airport as a suspected drug runner on his return from Cuba and Czechoslovakia, Ginsberg wrote to his congressman requesting he investigate the matter. Congressman Charles Joelson, Jr. in response to his inquiry, received a four-page report on Ginsberg from the U.S. Bureau of Narcotics. The report had incorporated, approvingly, Czechoslovakian files regarding Ginsberg's expulsion:

> ... GINSBERG, in his letter to Congressman [censored], stated that he had come back to New York after six months in Prague, Moscow, London, etc. Nowhere in this letter was it mentioned by GINSBERG that he was in fact expelled from Czechoslovakia. In an [censored] contained in our files, the [censored] quotes the May 16, 1965 issue of the Czechoslovakia publication *Mlada Fronta* in which an editorial appeared regarding GINSBERG, parts of which are quoted below.

> > 'Ginsberg's visit, instead of contributing to the recognition of cultural values created by leading American poets, has a negative effect because Ginsberg, in his extreme independence and irresponsibility, submits from his life those things which must be condemned: bisexuality, homosexuality, narcomania, alcoholism, posing, and a social extremism verging on orgies.' (Hyde, 244–245)

Beat Generation and then, just of himself. As recognizable as Charlie Chaplin was by his bowler hat, mustache, cane, and walk, so Ginsberg was signified by his beard, bald pate, and dark framed eye-glasses. Posters of him in an Uncle Sam hat or standing with Orlovsky, both naked and with their arms around each other, were ubiquitous. At their first meeting, Trungpa told Ginsberg to "take off your beard. I want to see your face. You're attached to your beard, aren't you?" That same evening, after trying to get away with just trimming it, Ginsberg shaved off his beard. "He took off his mask," Trungpa said upon seeing him. It was more than his beard that Ginsberg was attached to. It was the image of Allen Ginsberg that he projected because of his beard and casual garb. He found it both disturbing and liberating to walk around Berkeley without being recognized, clean shaven and in a suit and tie, which Trungpa also instructed should become his outfit after Ginsberg complained to him that he was not taken seriously as a poet. This change in appearance, however, quickly became part of Ginsberg's persona.

At that first meeting with Trungpa, Ginsberg complained, too, that he was tired because of the amount of traveling and by the number of readings he did. Trungpa told him it was because he did not like his poetry; he was bored with it; that he ought to improvise his readings, making up poetry on the spot. (Schumacher, 549–551) It was advice that extended the aesthetic principle that had been guiding Ginsberg since his first conversations with Kerouac, when they sought to express their consciousness in spontaneous expression. It had been the lesson he had learned from Neal Cassady's letter to Kerouac, which became the basis for Kerouac's spontaneous prose. And it continued what Bob Dylan had begun when he gave Ginsberg the money to buy a tape recorder so that he could dictate immediate poetry spontaneously. Trungpa also taught Ginsberg new techniques of meditation and, more important to Ginsberg, techniques of breath control and awareness.

The most difficult of Trungpa's teachings came wrapped in an altercation between him and the poet W.S. Merwin and Merwin's Japanese companion, Dana Naone, during a course in Buddhism Trungpa taught in Colorado. Ginsberg was not present. Trungpa's method as a Buddhist master was to put his students into a double bind: the disciple was maneuvered into a situation where there was only a choice of betrayals. Merwin, a well-established and well-known poet, Buddhist, and pacifist was in Colorado to deliver a series of lectures on Dante at The Jack Kerouac School of Disembodied Poetics. Ginsberg and Anne Waldman, the poet and coordinator of the poetry series at Saint Mark's Church in the Bowery on Manhattan's Lower East Side, had established the school at Trungpa's request at Naropa, a Buddhist university Trungpa founded in Colorado. As well as lecturing at Naropa, Merwin had enrolled in a seminar on Buddhism that Trungpa was offering. But there was tension. Merwin and Naone refused to chant some of the chants dedicated to the "Wrathful Dieties," the forces, according to Ginsberg, "which represent insight into human passion, aggression and ignorance, the 'three poisons." (Miles, 467) They felt that uttering such sentiments violated their pacifist principles. They told Trungpa of their reservations about the chants and about taking Buddhist vows. On the eve of Halloween, Trungpa declared there would be a party. Merwin and Naone stayed for an hour and then left. When Trungpa entered, he was, as he usually was, quite drunk. (Trungpa's drunkenness did not cause Ginsberg to discount wisdom or vision in him. Nor did a strongly aggressive personality like Trungpa's put him off. His mother, after all, remained always a beloved and wise person to him behind her mad persona. Jack Kerouac was always a saint and a guru to him. In even Kerouac's drunken or aggressive behavior and taunting or bigoted remarks, Ginsberg found wisdom to mine and accurate observation. Similarly with Burroughs—Ginsberg found him wise even as he might find him disturbing. That Trungpa was an alcoholic, thus, did not diminish his stature as a teacher for Ginsberg, nor did his authoritarianism.)

After Merwin and Naone had left the party, Trungpa summoned them to return. They refused when they saw that it was becoming bacchanalian. Trungpa had them brought forcibly to him despite their resistance, and ordered Merwin and Naone to take off their clothes. They refused. He asked them if they had something to hide and took off his own clothes and was carried around the room naked. After he had been dressed again, Trungpa ordered Merwin and Naone to be forcibly stripped. When they stood naked before him, Trungpa asked, "Was that so terrible?" and then accused Naone of being an Asian sex slave to a white man. The next day, it is reported, the three met and Merwin and Naone elected to stay on. What happened at that meeting or why they stayed after the Halloween party is not known.

Once news of this encounter began to spread, it was revealed that the incident actually involved Ginsberg more than the principals. As a disciple of Trungpa—whom he loved both romantically and for his life-long advocacy of liberty, spontaneity, and the sacredness of individual consciousness—Ginsberg was caught in a double bind. The question was whether he endorsed surrendering to what many saw as Trungpa's fascism or whether he would defend the liberty of will. He was called upon to take sides and felt a split loyalty. Characteristically, Ginsberg saw himself at fault either way, but understood there was a lesson of nonattachment to ego embodied in Trungpa's melodrama.

POLITICAL DEFIANCE

Neither Buddhist ceremonies and meditation nor his involvement with Naropa and the Kerouac School prevented Ginsberg from continuing an active involvement in other social and political events. In an unpublished poem, "To Marpa & Chogyam," he wrote

> What good is peace in my heart
> If other hearts burst with pain?
> What good my silent meditation
> If bombs scream down on Vietnam?
> I have no ecstasy in my head,
> filled with pictures of button bombs,
> I sigh "Sa" remembering my full belly
> while napalm flashes in New York Times. (Schumacher, 570)

Throughout the 1970s, therefore, Ginsberg found himself involved in a number of campaigns using his celebrity to focus attention on human issues of cultural, social, and political importance. He worked to free Timothy Leary, sentenced to 20 years on charges of marijuana possession. He also worked to get members of The Living Theater released from imprisonment in Brazil, again on marijuana charges, where the company had been organizing poor villagers by putting on plays with them. He also traveled to India in September 1971 to call attention to floods and famines that turned some seven million people into refugees. In 1972, Ginsberg participated in demonstrations at the Republican National Convention in Miami, protesting Richard Nixon's continuation of the Vietnam War, and afterwards gathered evidence proving that a violent confrontation, ostensibly started by some members of the Vietnam Veterans Against the War, was actually fomented by F.B.I. infiltrators seeking to give the demonstrators a bad image and get them arrested. Ginsberg was among those who spent several days in jail in Florida after a nonviolent sit-down demonstration at the convention protesting police brutality. In 1978, with Peter Orlovsky and Daniel Elsberg—who had worked in the U.S. government before he turned against the Vietnam War and leaked the *Pentagon Papers*—he sat down on railroad tracks to focus attention on the danger of nuclear energy by blocking the trains transporting plutonium.

nine

The Last Years

As I cross my kitchen floor the thought of death returns
—Allen Ginsberg, "May Day 1988"

CELEBRITY

Although Allen Ginsberg existed in the public imagination more as a cultural figure than as an active poet, he kept producing a steady flow of work. In 1970, Ferlinghetti published Ginsberg's *Indian Journals* from 1962 and 1963. In 1972, he published *The Fall of America: Poems of These States, 1965–1971*, a journal as poetry, composed as Ginsberg traveled across America, seeing its aspects and meditating on them as well as upon himself. *The Fall of America* won The National Book Award for Poetry. During the same year, a dramatization of his poem "Kaddish" played for a month at The Chelsea Theater in Brooklyn. In 1973, he was elected to the National Institute of Arts and Letters. In 1974, he wrote "Jahweh and Allah Battle" to undercut the conflict between Palestinians and Israelis. In 1976, he wrote "Father Death Blues" upon Louis's death at 80. In 1978, Ferlinghetti issued another Ginsberg collection in the City Lights Pocket Poet series, *Mind Breaths*. In July, when he was demonstrating against nuclear weaponry, Ginsberg wrote "Plutonian Ode," which became the title poem for his next collection, *Plutonian Ode: Poems 1977–1982*.

Ginsberg always had been a performing poet. "Howl" did not assert its existence on the page of a magazine or book, but through the reading Ginsberg did of it in San Francisco. In the 1970s he continued to perform, often with Bob Dylan's Rolling Thunder Review as it toured, and he did his own readings. In 1979, he went on a European tour with Living Theater musician Steven Taylor, Gregory Corso, and Orlovsky. In 1981, Ginsberg performed with the punk rock band, The Clash. In 1982, his record album, *First Blues* was released.

Ginsberg achieved international success without making the kind of money that generally accompanies such celebrity. He was poor for most of his life. He traveled extensively, but rather cheaply. Frequently, his trips were paid for, as when he went to

Chile, Cuba, Czechoslovakia, Vancouver, or India. He stayed in cheap hotels when he traveled, except when the host who invited him provided the accommodations, and his apartments in New York were on the Lower East Side, a poor, congested neighborhood of old tenements, whose vitality came from the folk cultures of the people, whether immigrants or Bohemians, who lived there. There he was mugged and wrote a poem about the incident. He generally bought his clothing secondhand from the Salvation Army. His father and his brother often loaned him money. When he bought his farm in upstate New York in 1968, Ginsberg went into debt for the first time.

Ginsberg's lack of money, however, was a deliberate choice. It reflected an antimaterialist, anticonsumption attitude. It also reflected loyalty and camaraderie, as in the case of his publisher. From the publication of *Howl* in 1956, for example, through the publication of *Plutonian Ode* in 1982, Ferlinghetti's City Lights was Ginsberg's publisher. City Lights, although it published handsome books, did not have the printing and distribution capabilities that larger publishing houses had. Consequently, Ginsberg's royalties from his books, which sold well, amounted to around $7,000 a year. Moreover, during those years, because of the limited resources of City Lights, a volume of Ginsberg's collected works, a sign of a poet's stature, recognition, and accomplishment, was never published.

When money did come to him, as from the Guggenheim award or from his public readings, which paid well, Ginsberg gave much of it away. And he often read for causes he believed in without pay. In 1966, his brother Gene established the Committee on Poetry, a foundation through which Ginsberg avoided paying taxes (refusing to help pay for the Vietnam War) and distributed "tens of thousands of dollars to small presses, underground newspapers, impoverished poets, and other projects, to further the cause of poetry." (Miles, 389)

In 1983 Ginsberg hired an agent, Andrew Wylie, who began organizing his affairs, for Ginsberg was, despite himself, a business. His poems were published in numerous magazines and his books were published throughout the world in many translated editions. He was regularly invited to read and to speak, and was often paid well for doing so. He was sought after to write introductions to other writers' books. He had an office and a staff. Bob Rosenthal ran Ginsberg's office, set his schedule, and made his appointments. Barry Miles, later his biographer organized all his tape-recorded songs and poems. Gordon Ball, who managed Ginsberg's farm, edited his journals for publication. Wylie secured a contract for Ginsberg with HarperCollins, and *Collected Poems, 1947–1980*, a volume of over 800 pages was published in 1984.

In 1982, Ginsberg traveled to Nicaragua to attend the Poetry Festival in Managua. Toward the end of 1979, an indigenous Nicaraguan insurgent force overthrew the U.S-installed and U.S.-supported dictatorship of Antonio Somoza. In response, the C.I.A.—working with pro-Somoza Nicaraguans in Miami—established an insurgent force, the Contras, to fight against the new socialist government of Nicaragua (called *Sandanista* after Augusto Sandino, who had led a fight against U.S. occupation of Nicaragua from 1926 to 1934, until defeated by Somoza's forces). The Poetry Festival was part of a literacy program being carried out by the Nicaraguan government and an attempt to show international solidarity with the revolutionary program at a time when the existence of the revolutionary program was threatened by American intervention. Aware that the Sandanistas were facing serious threats from the United States and mindful of his experiences in Cuba, Ginsberg met with Daniel Ortega, head of the Nicaraguan government, to discuss the issues important to him, like press censorship, and determined that *La Prensa*, which the Sandanistas had tried to shut down, was actually an instrument of the C.I.A. Ginsberg, Yevt-suchenko, and Nicaraguan poet Ernesto Cardinale issued a declaration calling for "liberty for Nicaragua independent of ambitions by either Cold War Superpower to dominate the Nicaraguan national scene." (Schumacher, 680)

In 1982, Ginsberg and Gary Snyder were part of a group of writers who met at UCLA with a delegation of writers from The People's Republic of China to begin forging cultural ties between China and the United States. It had only been 10 years since Richard Nixon had gone to China, met with Mao-Tse Tung and Zhou Enlai, and given China diplomatic recognition. It had been only five years since the end of the Cultural Revolution, a period of intense violence, disorder, humiliation, torture, and cultural nihilism that Mao had set in motion in the 1960s. Two years after that meeting, a group of American writers was invited to China to continue the literary dialogue, and Ginsberg and Snyder were part of it. Ginsberg was surprised to discover the extent to which his work was known in China and how much influence his poetry had on some contemporary Chinese poets. In China, too, without incident, he spoke publicly and privately of individual issues like sexuality in the face of the social prohibitions.

In 1988, Ginsberg traveled to Israel. Before a rally of 60,000 people gathered in Tel Aviv to protest the treatment of Palestinians in Israeli occupied territory, Ginsberg read "Jaweh and Allah Battle." When he returned to the United States he helped compose a letter by the P.E.N. Freedom-to-Write Committee calling for the Israeli government to stop censoring Palestinian and Israeli writers, to reopen newspapers that had been shut down, and to allow books and newspapers to circulate freely.

Towards the end of 1989, after the Soviet Union renounced its empire and its puppet states became autonomous, Ginsberg returned to Prague. This time, rather than being expelled, he was greeted by the republic's new president, the dissident poet and activist Vaclav Havel.

The last years of Ginsberg's life followed the same pattern as all the preceding years; Ginsberg showed hardly any sign of slowing down. He bore the marks of certain illnesses: cirrhosis

Eschewing Sexual Classification

The following anecdote and commentary were reported by Al Aronowitz, the journalist who wrote *The New York Post* series of articles on the Beat generation in the late 1950s:

"In Chicago once, a woman asked Allen Ginsberg 'Mr. Ginsberg, why is it that you have so much homosexuality in your poetry?'

'Because,' Ginsberg replied, 'I'm queer.'

But that was only half an answer.

'I sleep,' he has since said 'with men and with women. I am neither queer nor not queer nor am I bisexual. My name is Allen Ginsberg and I sleep with whoever I want.'

'I don't know whether it's a great sociological problem or not,' he says. 'Most of the poets are not queer, actually. Some are. But it's not homosexuality — I don't like the term because here in America it immediately brings in a whole sociological frame of reference, a whole psychological frame of reference. And bisexual, that has sort of a corny connotation, too. Like I'm making it with women, lots of people do. I'm a lover. Another thing: I think that it's pretty shameful that in this culture people have to be so frightened of their own normal sex lives and are frightened of other people knowing about it to the point where they have to go slinking around making ridiculous tragedies of their lives. So it seems for one thing, at this point, that it's necessary for the poets to speak out directly about intimate matters, if they come into the poetry, which they do in mine, and not attempt to hide them or evade the issues. Life is full of strange experiences.'"

(*www.bigmagic.com/pages/blackj/column25.html*)

of the liver, hepatitis, diabetes, and Bell's palsy—which left his face partially paralyzed and accounted for one of his eyes becoming narrower than the other. His relationship with Orlovsky, while maintaining its subterranean strength of connection, nevertheless on the surface became more distant. Orlovsky's alcoholic and psychotic episodes continued, and the two lived apart. Perhaps Ginsberg mellowed a little. His use of psychotropic pharmacology decreased and he relied on meditation rather than morphine or LSD for transcendence, but he continued to smoke marijuana. He continued his Buddhist studies and his teaching at Naropa until 1986, when he was appointed Distinguished Professor of Poetry at Brooklyn College. When he sold his papers to Stanford for one million dollars in 1994, he bought a loft on the Lower East Side, where he had an apartment, and furnished it comfortably. Acceptance, inclusion, and respectability were conferred on Ginsberg without forcing him to deviate from the ways and beliefs that had first propelled him in the 1940s.

In July 1994, he was honored by a weeklong seminar at Naropa, "Beats and Other Rebel Angels." Guests assembled in tribute included the poets Ferlinghetti, Snyder, Corso, Robert Creely, Ann Waldman, Galway Kinnell, and Amiri Baraka; musicians and performers Meredith Monk and David Amram; and Dave Dellinger, the pacifist activist.

DEATH

The paradox of Allen Ginsberg's life was the result of a conflict at the root of his creativity. It was a conflict between life and death, between desire and detachment, between ego and oblivion, between awareness *of* what is and awareness *that* what is is nothing, and that "nothing" itself must be considered sacred. Ginsberg accepted Blake's credo that everything that lives is holy and simultaneously he accepted the Buddhist wisdom that everything is transient, illusory, and must be let go, and that its transience, in fact, is the source of its holiness. Awareness, then, the faculty cultivated by meditation, is primarily an awareness of transience and emptiness. Awareness is the practice of having and releasing simultaneously.

The negotiation of these contraries defined the pattern of Ginsberg's life. He sought fame for himself and his friends with an unrelenting energy and the savvy of a person who has had a career in marketing. At the same time, his quest, whether through drugs or meditation, was self-obliteration and the experience of transience.

Allen Ginsberg died on April 6, 1997 of liver cancer. If the manner of his death is any indication, he succeeded in his quest to value life and yet to see it as illusion, transient and nonexistent. He learned of the cancer a week before his death and was told by his doctor that he had between four months and a year to live, but Ginsberg told Bob Rosenthal, he thought it much less. "I thought I would be terrified," Ginsberg told Burroughs over the phone, "in fact I am exhilarated." (Caveny, 202) He made hundreds of phone calls from his bed to say goodbye to friends and he wrote the poem, "Things I'll Not Do."

Ginsberg slipped into unconsciousness on April 3, 1997, three days before his death. "Allen lay on a narrow hospital bed beside the windows overlooking 14th Street.... two almost invisible tubes coming out of his nose attached to a portable oxygen tank.... [T]hrough the loft people whispering greetings, hugging, telling ... all that had happened.... An altar ... along one side of the loft ... and ... [Buddhist] monks sat chanting and praying ... bells tinkling." (Caveny, 203)

Ginsberg's body was cremated and "the ashes were divided. One portion went to be poured into the foundation of a rest area at the Rocky Mountain Shambala Center in Colorado. An equal portion was given to Galek Rinpoche [Ginsberg's

Buddhist teacher]. The rest of the ashes [were] buried in the family plot in Elizabeth, New Jersey, right next to his father." (Caveny, 208)

afterword

When Allen Ginsberg died it was the first time in my life
that I thought there must be life after death because he has
to go somewhere. With everyone else it was just tragic. But
with him it was, Okay, what now?
                    —Exene Cervenkova, *The Rolling Stone*
                                        Book of the Beats

CRITICAL RESPONSE

The work of Allen Ginsberg since he burst onto the scene at The Six Gallery with "Howl" has generated a large body of criticism and continues to do so. A web search, for example, of the Modern Language Association's bibliography brings up more than 200 entries for Ginsberg. As with all poets, he has his admirers and detractors, and of course critics disagree about the merits of particular works. Michael Shechner, for example, finds that the poems in *Mind Breaths* are 'like refrains from earlier books," but "far less inspired," than Ginsberg's "pure breath, biomusic ... does not translate easily into words." (Hyde, 333) Writing of the same volume, Hayden Carruth called the poems in *Mind Breaths* "a marvel ... good as anything he has ever written." He described them as "poems of the imagination, poems arising from within, complexes of feeling that come to consciousness with their own structure already in them." (Hyde, 321, 322) Nevertheless, Alan Brownjohn's 1969 assertion that as a poet, "Allen Ginsberg has always somehow slipped out of the grasp of criticism" is perhaps the singularly most reliable critical observation that can be made about Ginsberg's work.

Allen Ginsberg's poetry, as it appeared, was a social phenomenon that existed very much in the context of the persona of the poet. By presenting his voice, breath, biography, politics, and spiritual and psychological struggles, his poetry simply presented the man Ginsberg himself, the world around him as he perceived it, and an aspect, larger or smaller, defined or inchoate, of his readers' fears or desires. Once they came into existence his poems simply existed as Ginsberg himself did, as part of American culture and consciousness. They were entries, forces actually, in the culture wars that Pat Buchanan, the conservative political commentator and activist, said were being waged for the spirit of America. The strength of the presence of

Ginsberg's poems was not a function of learned, critical, or academic response to them. Criticism came after the poetry rather than heralding it. So did the academy, which recognized and rewarded Ginsberg—the poet who began his career in opposition to the academy and whose linguistic candor, political and cultural radicalism, and homosexual Bohemian way of living never conformed to its decorum.

The critical response to Allen Ginsberg's poetry, moreover, was for the most part a response to the values it celebrated and the attitude of the poet to the world out of which his poetry was generated. The criticism was as much a reflection of the temperament and disposition of the critics toward the kind of life Allen Ginsberg lived, and to the political and cultural values he advocated and that his poetry reflected, as it was an evaluation of independent textual works. William Carlos Williams, in a note to Marianne Moore asking her to look at Ginsberg's poetry, wrote that "I'm instinctively drawn to him," and that "I have a strange feeling of exceptional sensitivity [in Ginsberg] that is almost lost." He is speaking of the man more than of the poetry. Moore responded similarly, despite herself. Writing to Ginsberg, she reminded him, "In the opening piece … you say, 'I wandered off in search of a toilet.' And I go with you, remember. Do I have to? I do if you take me with you in your book." (Hyde, 12–13) After similar objections, Moore concludes "Why do I say all this? Because your trials, your own realness, and capacity affect me." Richard Eberhart's 1956 piece in the *The New York Times Book Review*, the essay that reported what had already happened, examined "Howl" as a social document as well as a poem and Ginsberg as a cultural phenomenon as well as a poet. Suddenly, it appeared, people who made poetry also made news. John Hollander, scholar and poet, writing half a year later in *Partisan Review* called *Howl* "a dreadful little volume" with an "utter lack of decorum of any kind." But rather than being a criticism of the poem, Hollander's essay reflects an uneasy attitude towards the poem. As does M.L. Rosenthal's 1957 review in *The Nation,* which described Ginsberg as writing with "the single-minded frenzy of a raving madwoman." In his rebuttal, Kenneth Rexroth asserted—this is not an argument about poetry, notice—"It is Hollywood or the censors who are obscene. It is [United States Secretary of State under Eisenhower, John Foster] Dulles and [Soviet Premier, Nikita] Khrushchev who are childishly defiant. It is the 'media' that talk with the single minded frenzy of a raving madwoman." After more cultural argument and assertion that Ginsberg's poetry is really echoing Auden's prescription that "we must love one another or die," Rexroth turns to poetics: "Ginsberg is one of the most remarkable versifiers in American.... almost alone in his ... ability to make powerful poetry of the inherent rhythms of our speech." Rexroth's closing prophecy, "that if he keeps going, Ginsberg will be the first genuinely popular, genuine poet in over a generation" proved true, and also provided the reason that Ginsberg defied criticism. His poetry generated its audience by being able to fit into the common speech and reflect common perception and common discontent.

Ginsberg did not function within the American university and academic system. He did not rely on magazines to publish his poems, although they did. He was a personality; a performer; an example of sexual, emotional, and intellectual candor; and a role model. He was a political and cultural presence like his friends in The Living Theater, Julian Beck and Judith Malina; like the social critic, novelist, poet and 1960s youth guru, Paul Goodman; like the poet and activist Ed Sanders of the rock group, *The Fugs;* or like peace activists and organizers Abbie Hoffman and Dave Dellinger.

As much as he wished to obliterate ego, Ginsberg existed as an image, as a poster—indeed, as several different posters—that were ubiquitous in the 1960s and 1970s. His work constitutes a biography of himself, a history of his time, and an intervention designed to restore love and peace to a global consciousness Ginsberg saw as painfully corrupted. And just as his work and his persona generated an enthusiastic audience whose lives were changed by them or who saw themselves or their beliefs, fears, and dreams reflected in them, so they also generated antipathy

Women in the Beat Generation

Stephen Scobie, who has written about Leonard Cohen, Jacques Derrida, and Bob Dylan, reported the following exchange on the presence of women in the Beat generation. The occasion was a celebration of Allen Ginsberg's life at Naropa in 1994.

Corso is genially drunk, interrupting everyone with inapposite remarks. Then a woman from the audience asks: 'Why are there so few women on this panel? Why are there so few women in this whole week's program? Why were there so few women among the Beat writers?' and Corso, suddenly utterly serious, leans forward and says: 'There were women, they were there, I knew them, their families put them in institutions, they were given electric shock. In the 50s if you were male you could be a rebel, but if you were female your families had you locked up. There were cases, I knew them, someday someone will write about them'.... Then Gregory is back to the clown mode: 'Why aren't we more celebrated? In Europe they name streets after poets, why not in America? Why shouldn't there be an Allen Ginsberg Street in San Francisco?' 'But Gregory,' says Allen, 'there are streets named after you all over Italy: Corso ... Corso ...'"

(www.litkicks.com/Topics/NaropaReport.html)

among those whose political and cultural preferences were different from Ginsberg's. Selden Rodman, for example, writing in the conservative *National Review*, vilifies Ginsberg, saying,

> There is not a trace of passion or tenderness in the homosexual encounters he describes with clinically repulsive detail. His hatred of America and his reiterated complaint that the CIA exists to subvert good government abroad, carry no more supportive evidence than the well-known statement at the beginning of "Howl" that his mentally deranged friends are the "best minds" of his generation. (Hyde, 330)

Jeffrey Hart, another *National Review* contributor, wrote a similar evaluation of Ginsberg's work, except, he knew Ginsberg and emphasizes throughout his essay that

> to my further surprise, I found that Allen was actually good company and that I rather liked him. We took to having lunch once in a while, favoring Paone's Italian restaurant, a sort of *National Review* hangout. The rather macho waiters had to get used to Allen bringing some food of his own, several kinds of rice, some dry fish and so on. He told me he had to be careful because of diabetes, and lined up a row of pills on the table. His blood pressure was bad, too. You just had to accept the fact that with Allen things were always going to be a bit out of the ordinary. His manner was very sweet and paternal.
> (*www.dartreview.com/archives/2000/09/18/learning_to_like_allen_ginsberg.php*)

Ginsberg forced his way into mainstream consciousness and academic consideration because of his tenacious grip on the popular imagination and his unwavering adherence to

Bohemian values and his candid ambivalence about his own success. Ginsberg did not pursue the kind of success that his Columbia classmate and nemesis Norman Podhoretz, the neo-conservative editor of *Commentary* magazine did, and called "making it." Ginsberg pursued the integrity of Allen Ginsberg, as it was accomplished through poetry, in a struggle—which was the subject of his poetry— between identity and illusion, carried out within a world he saw organized to deny both material and spiritual humanity.

HIS LEGACY

Writing in *The New Yorker* in 1996, in a review subtitled, "Forty years of Allen Ginsberg's poetry," Helen Vendler is confident that Ginsberg's poetry "will enter the matrix of tradition," that he "has added something new." He has continued to explore "the texture of consciousness," by exploring "the unspeakable (his mother's vomiting and defecating in the bathroom in "Kaddish," his own sexual groveling in "Please Master," his embarrassment at the effects of Bell's palsy in "What You Up To?")." (Vendler, 99, 100) The sensibility that disturbed Marianne Moore in the early 1950s has become the element that is revelatory for Vendler at the century's end.

Nevertheless, it may be too early to judge Allen Ginsberg's legacy as a poet and his place in the literary tradition. First, his human presence must dissolve and his textual presence must predominate. And even then, the course that history, culture, and politics take will influence—undoubtedly more strongly than with many other poets—the way his poetry is approached and seen. It is certain, however, that Ginsberg's influence on poetry, consciousness, and actual life choices, no matter what the critical fate of his poetry, has been overwhelming during his lifetime. At the same time, it is important to realize the inevitable reciprocity that existed between Ginsberg and his time. He was as much enabled by his era as he influenced it. At a time when a revolt against many of society's traditional institutions and the order they enforced or enhanced was beginning, Allen Ginsberg brought the bardic, minstrel, romantic, and magical aspects of poetry forward to challenge a poetry of reserve and intellectual discipline.

As a collaborator in the Beat Generation of the 1950s and the Hippie movement of the 1960s, Ginsberg exerted a strong influence on the way countless young people chose to live. Not only a poet of the stage as well as the page, Ginsberg was a communal poet. His work was part of the Beat movement he began with Kerouac, Burroughs, Leroy Jones, and others, and his influence extended beyond poets of the page to the generation of folk poets like Bob Dylan, Phil Ochs, Eric Andersen, Tim Buckley, Jim Morrison, Patti Smith, Chuck D., Bono, and others. According to Lou Reed, poet and singer, "Modern rock lyrics would be inconceivable without the work of Allen Ginsberg." (*Rolling Stone* 278)

Ginsberg has written that "the original task" of his work "was to 'widen the area of consciousness' make pragmatic examination of the texture of consciousness, even somewhat transform consciousness." (Vendler, 99) And he did, by moving myriad young people, from the 1950s onward, away from allegiance to middle-class decorum and stability. He achieved this through his poetry, his prose, and his public appearances; through his open homosexuality before the era of Gay Liberation; through his advocacy of marijuana and LSD; and through his fierce and witty opposition to war, the money system, secret government operations, and State control of consciousness, whether exercised by Capitalist democracies or Communist dictatorships.

Ball, Gordon, ed. *Journals: Early Fifties Early Sixties.* New York: Grove Press, 1977.

Caveney, Graham. *Screaming With Joy: The Life of Allen Ginsberg.* New York: Broadway Books, Random House, 1999.

George-warren, Holly, ed. *The Rolling Stone Book of the Beats: The Beat Generation and American Culture.* New York: Hyperion, 1999.

Ginsberg, Allen. *Collected Poems, 1947–1980.* New York: Harper & Row, 1984.

———. *Cosmopolitan Greetings: Poems, 1986–1992.* New York: Harper-Collins, 1994.

Glick, Nathan. "The Last Great Critic." *The Atlantic Monthly* Vol. 286, No. 1 (2000): 86–90.

Kramer, Jane. "Paterfamilias—I." *The New Yorker* (August 17, 1968): 32.

———. "Paterfamilias—II." *The New Yorker* (August 24, 1968): 38.

Miles, Barry. *Ginsberg.* New York: Simon and Schuster, 1989.

Schumacher, Michael. *Dharma Lion: A Critical Biography of Allen Ginsberg.* New York: St. Martin's Press, 1992.

———, ed. *Family Business: Selected Letters between a Father and Son.* London: Bloomsbury, 2002.

Stoehr, Taylor, ed. "The Politics of Being Queer," in *Nature Heals: The Psychological Essays of Paul Goodman.* New York: E.P. Dutton, 1979, 216.

Vendler, Helen. "American X-Rays: Forty years of Allen Ginsberg's poetry." *The New Yorker* (November 4, 1996): 98.

Williams, William Carlos. *Spring & All.* Frontier Press, 1970.

1926   Ginsberg is born, June 3, in Newark, New Jersey.

1929   Naomi Ginsberg (mother) has pancreatic operation and subsequent mental breakdown.

1930–34   Naomi active in Communist Party U.S.A.; takes Ginsberg to party meetings; spend summers at party camp.

1935   Naomi suffers a series of mental breakdowns. Louis Ginsberg (father) commits her to Greystone State Mental Hospital.

1936   Naomi returns home, but is subject to paranoid delusions.

1937   On June 24 Naomi attempts suicide behind locked bathroom door. Louis breaks door down. Naomi committed to Greystone for two years. Ginsberg, age 11, begins keeping diary.

1939   Ginsberg graduates from elementary school in June. Begins attending Paterson Central High in the fall. Becomes president of Debating Club. Naomi returns home after two years in mental hospital.

1941   Ginsberg hears Walt Whitman for first time in September when Miss Durbin, English teacher, reads to his class. In December Naomi suffers relapse, compels Ginsberg to take her on long bus ride to rest home and commit her. She is disruptive. Louis is called next morning and is forced to recommit her to Greystone.

1942   Allen's brother Eugene is in the military stationed in Great Britain. Ginsberg works on congressional campaign for local labor organizer in October.

1943   Graduates high school. Begins attending Columbia University on scholarship in the fall. Meets Lucien Carr, David Kammerer, and William S. Burroughs in December.

1944   In June Ginsberg meets Jack Kerouac. On August 14 Lucien Carr kills David Kammerer.

1945   Burroughs meets Herbert Huncke and introduces him to Ginsberg in January. They start exploring the underbelly of Manhattan. On March 16, Ginsberg is suspended from Columbia. Moves into Joan Vollmer's apartment, where he lives with Burroughs, Kerouac, Huncke, and others. Joins Merchant Marines on August 1. Graduates in November. Ships out on first voyage. On board with crewmates, first time he smokes marijuana.

1946   Returns to Columbia in September. Meets Neal Cassady in December.

1947   In January Burroughs and Joan Vollmer move to Texas to grow marijuana. Huncke joins them. In July Ginsberg visits Neal Cassady in Denver. Both travel to Texas to visit Burroughs and Joan Vollmer. Ginsberg ships out from Gaveston for Dakar with the Merchant Marines in September and returns to New York City a month later. In November, with Ginsberg's consent, Naomi is given a lobotomy.

1948   Ginsberg has an audio-vision of William Blake reading "Ah, Sunflower" in July.

1949   Herbert Huncke moves into Ginsberg's apartment in February and begins using it as a place to store stolen goods. In April Ginsberg is arrested, appearing to be part of a burglary ring; he pleads insanity and enters Columbia Psychiatric Institute, where he meets Carl Solomon.

1950   Ginsberg released from Columbia Psychiatric on February 27. Lives with father and stepmother, Edith, in Paterson, New Jersey and holds a series of "straight" jobs; attempts to lead a heterosexual sex life. On March 30 Ginsberg hears William Carlos Williams read at the Guggenheim Museum. Two days later, Ginsberg writes to him. Ginsberg meets Gregory Corso.

1951   At Ginsberg's urging, Ace Books contracts to publish Kerouac's *On the Road* in December.

1952   Ginsberg takes peyote for the first time in April.

1953   In May, at Ginsberg's urging, Ace contracts to publish Burroughs's novel *Junkie*. Burroughs moves in with

Ginsberg and Corso in September; Ginsberg and Burroughs become lovers. By December Ginsberg ends sexual relations with Burroughs, who goes to Tangier. Ginsberg goes to Mexico, stays six months.

1954   Ginsberg arrives in San Francisco in June. In December Ginsburg meets and falls in love with Peter Orlovsky.

1955   Ginsberg writes first and last parts of "Howl" in August. In September Ginsberg meets Philip Whalen and Gary Snyder. Writes "Sunflower Sutra" and "A Supermarket in California." On October 13, Ginsberg reads "Howl" at the Six Gallery.

1956   Naomi dies of brain hemorrhage at Greystone State Mental Hospital on June 9. From July to September Ginsberg signs on to a Navy ship as a yeoman storekeeper delivering supplies to the Arctic Circle. In October *Howl and Other Poems* is published by City Lights.Along with Orlovsky brothers and Corso, Ginsberg visits Kerouac in Mexico in November. They all travel by car to New York.

1957   In March Ginsberg and Orlovsky leave for Morocco, meet Burroughs there. Ginsberg works on *Naked Lunch* with Burroughs. City Lights Bookstore clerk Shig Murao and store owner Lawrence Ferlinghetti are arrested for selling *Howl and Other Poems* to two undercover policemen on May 21. In June Ginsberg and Orlovsky leave Morocco, travel through Spain, arrive in Paris, where they stay for 10 months, are joined by Corso. Judge Clayton Horn rules that *Howl* is not obscene on October 3. In November, in a café in Paris, Ginsberg begins writing "Kaddish."

1958   Neal Cassady is arrested for possession of two marijuana joints on April 8; does 26 months in San Quentin prison. Ginsberg sails from France to New York on July 17.

1959   Ginsberg reads "Kaddish" to an overflowing crowd at Columbia University's McMillan Theater on February 5. In May, at Stanford University's Mental Research

Institute, under the supervision of Gregory Bateson, Ginsberg takes LSD for the first time.

1960   Ginsberg and Ferlinghetti attend literary conference in Chile. Ginsberg travels through Bolivia and Peru and tries the hallucinogenic plant yage. Ginsberg takes psilocybin under Timothy Leary's supervison on November 26.

1961   Ginsberg begins a trip on March 23 that will last more than two years and take him to Paris, Tangier, Nairobi, India, Vietnam, Cambodia, and Japan. On April 29 *Kaddish and Other Poems* is published.

1963   Ginsberg writes "The Change" on a train from Kyoto to Tokyo on May 15. On July 17 Ginsberg participates in poetry conference in Vancouver, British Columbia. In November Ginsberg moves from San Francisco back to New York City.

1964   Ginsberg, Corso, and Orlovsky tour New England. Ginsberg's reading of "Kaddish" at Brandeis is recorded and released as a record.

1965   Ginsberg testifies in defense of *Naked Lunch* at an obscenity trial in Boston on January 11. Ginsberg travels to Cuba and Czechoslovakia from January to May— where he is crowned King of the May on May Day—and is expelled from both countries for his outspokenness. Visits mother's relatives in Moscow. On May 9, in London, Ginsberg organizes a poetry reading with Bob Dylan and meets The Beatles. Organizes an international poetry reading at the Albert Hall on June 11, which draws an audience of 7,000. Ginsberg is strip-searched by U.S. Customs agents upon returning to the United States on June 29. Reads at the Berkeley Poetry Conference. Afterwards, backpacks to Oregon and Washington State with Gary Snyder. Mediates between peace activists and Hell's Angels in Berkeley in October; begins year of "flower power."

1966   Forms the Committee on Poetry on March 26 in order to donate his earnings to needy poets and avoid paying taxes to the U.S. government and supporting the Vietnam War. Testifies before the U.S. Senate Judiciary Subcommittee on Juvenile Delinquency against making the possession of LSD illegal on June 14.

1967 On January 14, Ginsberg is one of the principal organizers of the Human Be-In in San Francisco. Reads at the Spoleto Festival in Italy on July 5 and is briefly detained by the Italian police for the "use of certain words." On July 20, participates in the "Dialectics of Liberation" conference organized by R.D. Laing in London. His talk is called "Consciousness and Practical Action." Travels through Wales afterwards, takes LSD there, and writes "Wales Visitation." Ginsberg meets Ezra Pound on October 28 and talks about poetry and Pound's career. Pound tells him he repents of his antisemitism. Ginsberg arrested on December 5 during antidraft demonstrations in Manhattan.

1968 Neal Cassady dies February 3. In July Ginsberg buys an 80-acre farm in upstate New York. From August 24–30 Ginsberg in Chicago for Democratic National Convention. In November *Planet News* published.

1969 Records his settings of Blake songs in June for The Beatles Apple Records. Songs are released in 1970 by MGM records. Jack Kerouac dies October 21. In December Ginsberg testifies for the defense at the trial of the Chicago 8, organizers of the protest at the Democratic National Convention. Prosecutor calls him a "faggot."

1970 In August Ginsberg meets Tibetan Lama Chogyam Trungpa, Rinpoche, who becomes his guru.

1971 Visiting India and West Bengal in September, Ginsberg tours refugee camps and observes results of floods and famine. Writes "September on Jessore Road." Records First Blues with Bob Dylan in November. Album is released in 1983.

1972 In January "Kaddish" staged at the Chelsea Theater in Brooklyn. Arrested at Republican National Convention in Florida in August after demonstration is disrupted by F.B.I. infiltrators. The Fall of America is published in December; receives the National Book Award for Poetry.

1973   Ginsberg is elected to the National Institute of Arts and Letters in February. Goes on a meditation retreat in Wyoming with Trungpa from September to December; writes "Mind Breaths."

1974   Writes "Jaweh and Allah Battle" on January 13. In the spring, at Trangpa's request, along with Anne Waldman, Ginsberg founds the Jack Kerouac School of Disembodied Poetics at Naropa in Boulder, Colorado.

1975–1976   Ginsberg is part of Bob Dylan's Rolling Thunder Concert Tour.

1976   Louis Ginsberg dies July 7.

1978   On January 1, City Lights publishes *Mind Breaths*. Ginsberg, Daniel Ellsberg, and Orlovsky protest nuclear proliferation by sitting down on railroad tracks in Colorado and blocking trains carrying plutonium. Ginsberg arrested twice. Writes "Plutonian Ode."

1979   Ginsberg reads and sings on a tour of Europe.

1981   June 10, performs "Capitol Air" on stage with The Clash and performs "Ghetto Defendant" on their album, *Combat Rock*. In October Ginsberg moves to Boulder, Colorado, to direct Kerouac School of Disembodied Poetics at Naropa.

1982   *Plutonian Ode* is published January 1, the last volume of his poetry to be published by Ferlinghetti's City Lights Books.Ginsberg participates in Poetry Conference in Nicaragua sponsored by the Sandanistas, meets with Daniel Ortega, president of Nicaragua's revolutionary government. In July, at Naropa, Ginsberg hosts 25th anniversary celebration of the publication of Kerouac's *On the Road*.

1983   *First Blues* record album released.

1984	As part of an American Academy of Arts & Letters delegation, Ginsberg participates in a four-day writers' conference in Beijing in October and travels through parts of China for two months more.
1985	As part of a six-book, six-figure deal arranged by his newly hired agent, Andrew Wylie, Harper & Row publishes Ginsberg's *Collected Poems, 1947–1980.* "Hideous Human Angels," an exhibition of Ginsberg's photography opens at the Holly Solomon Gallery in Manhattan.
1986	Ginsberg moves back to New York City after being appointed Distinguished Professor of English at Brooklyn College.
1987	Chogyam Trungpa, Rinpoche dies April 4. In August Ginsberg records *The Lion for Real,* a poetry and music album.
1989	Collaborates with composer Philip Glass on *Wichita Vortex Sutra* and *Hydrogen Jukebox.*
1990	Twelve Trees Press publishes a book of Ginsberg's photography.
1994	Four-CD collection of recorded songs, *Holy Soul Jelly Roll* released. Celebration of his career at Naropa. Sells archives to Stanford University. Buys a loft on Lower East Side, New York. *Cosmopolitan Greetings* published.
1997	Ginsberg dies at home of liver cancer on April 5.

WORKS BY ALLEN GINSBERG

POETRY

Howl and Other Poems (1956)

Kaddish and Other Poems (1961)

Reality Sandwiches (1963)

Planet News (1968)

The Gates of Wrath. Rhymed Poems 1948–51 (1972)

The Fall of America. Poems of These States (1973)

Iron Horse (1974)

Mind Breaths. Poems 1971–76 (1978)

Plutonian Ode. Poems 1977–1980 (1982)

Collected Poems 1947–1980 (1984)

Howl Annotated (1986) with facsimile manuscript

White Shroud Poems 1980–1985 (1986)

Cosmopolitan Greetings. Poems 1986–1992 (1994)

Illuminated Poems (1996) illustrated by Eric Drooker

Selected Poems 1947–1995 (1996)

PROSE

The yage Letters (1963) with William S. Burroughs

Indian Journals (1970)

Allen Verbatim: Lectures on Poetry etc. (1974)

Gay Sunshine Interview (1974) with Allen Young

Chicago Trial Testimony (1975)

To Eberhart from Ginsberg (1976)

As Ever: Collected Correspondence of Allen Ginsberg & Neal Cassady (1977)

Journals Early Fifties Early Sixties (1977)

Composed on the Tongue. Literary Conversations 1967–1977 (1980)

Straight Hearts' Delight: Love Poems and Selected Letters (1980) with Peter Orlovsky

Your Reason and Blake's System (1988)

Journals Mid-Fifties (1995)

Family Business: Selected Letters Between a Father and Son: Allen and Louis Ginsberg (2001)

BOOKS OF PHOTOGRAPHY

Allen Ginsberg & Robert Frank (1985)

Allen Ginsberg Fotografier 1947–87 (1987)

Reality Sandwiches (1989)

Allen Ginsberg Photographs (1991)

Snapshot Poetics (1993)

Allen Ginsberg 108 Images (1995)

SPOKEN WORD: RECORDINGS

Howl and Other Poems (1959)

Kaddish (1966)

Ginsberg's Thing (1969)

Wm. Blake's Songs of Innocence & Experience (1970) tuned by Allen Ginsberg

Mind Breaths & Other Poems Early Seventies (1976)

Allen Ginsberg In Wuppertal (1980)

Gaté. Songs of the Seventies (1980)

Gaté. Two evenings with Allen Ginsberg (1980)

Birdbrain (1981)

First Blues. Rags, Ballads & Harmonium Songs (1981)

German Tour. Poems & Songs late Seventies (1981)

Howl & Later Poems (1981)

A Little Bit Of Awareness (1981)

Plutonian Ode & Other Poems Late Seventies (1981)

First Blues: Songs 1975–1981 (1983)

September on Jessore Road (1983)

Made In Texas (1986)

May 22, 1986 (1986)

Hobo (1987)

The Lion For Real (1989)

Beauty and The Beast (1991)

Howls, Raps & Roars (1993)

Holy Soul Jelly Roll. Poems & Songs 1949–1993 (1994)

The Ballad Of The Skeleton (1996)

MUSICAL COMPOSITIONS BASED ON GINSBERG'S POETRY

Hydrogen Jukebox (1993)

Cosmopolitan Greetings. Jazzy Opera (1993)

Howl, U S A (1996)

Aiken, William. "Denise Levertov, Robert Duncan, and Allen Ginsberg: Modes of the Self in Projective Poetry." *Modern Poetry Studies* 10.2/3 (1981): 200–245.

Breslin, James. "Allen Ginsberg: The Origins of 'Howl' and 'Kaddish.'" *Iowa Review* 8.2 (Spring 1977): 82–108.

Breslin, Paul. "Allen Ginsberg as Representative Man: The Road to Naropa." *The Psycho-Political Muse: American Poetry Since The Fifties.* Chicago: University of Chicago Press, 1987: 22–41.

Burns, Glen. *Great Poets Howl: A Study of Allen Ginsberg's Poetry, 1943–1955.* Grove/Atlantic, 1983.

Caveney, Graham. *Screaming with Joy: The Life of Allen Ginsberg.* New York: Broadway Books, 1999.

Clark, Thomas. "Allen Ginsberg: An Interview." *Paris Review*, 10 (Spring 1966): 13–55.

Dougherty, Jay. "From Society to Self: Ginsberg's Inward Turn in 'Mind Breaths.'" *Sagetrieb* 6.1 (Spring 1987): 81–92.

Dowden, George. *A Bibliography of Works by Allen Ginsberg, October 1943 To July 1, 1967.* San Francisco: City Lights Books, 1971.

Edwards, Susan, and Cindy L. Carr. *The Wild West Wind: Remembering Allen Ginsberg.* Boulder, Colorado: Baksun Books, 2001.

Faas, Ekbert. "Allen Ginsberg." *Towards a New American Poetics.* Santa Barbara: Black Sparrow, 1979: 269–288.

Geneson, Paul. "A Conversation with Allen Ginsberg." *Chicago Review* (Summer 1975).

Gertmenian, Donald. "Remembering and Rereading 'Howl.'" *Ploughshares*, 2 (1975): 151–163.

Ginsberg, Allen. "Ginsberg." *Intrepid.* 18/19 (1971): 52–61.

Hahn, Stephen. "The Prophetic Voice of Allen Ginsberg." *Prospectus: Annual of American Cultural Studies*, 2 (1976): 527–567.

Heffernan, James. "Politics and Freedom: Refractions of Blake in Joyce Cary and Allen Ginsberg." *Romantic and Modern*, ed. George Bornstein. Pittsburgh: University of Pittsburgh Press, 1977.

Howard, Richard. "Allen Ginsberg." *Alone With America: Essays on the Art of Poetry in the United States Since 1950*. NY: Atheneum, 1980: 176–183.

Hyde, Lewis, ed. *On the Poetry of Allen Ginsberg*. Ann Arbor: University of Michigan Press, 1984.

Kerouac, Jack. "Allen Ginsberg," (Portraits: Writers anecdotes about other writers). *The Paris Review* v. 29 (Winter 1987): 212.

Koch, Kenneth. "Allen Ginsberg Talks About Poetry." *New York Times Book Review* 23 (October 1977): 9, 44–46.

Kramer, Jane. *Allen Ginsberg in America: With a New Introduction by the Author*. New York: Fromm International, 1997.

Kraus, Michelle. *Allen Ginsberg: An Annotated Bibliography, 1969–1977*. Metuchen, NJ: Scarecrow Press, 1980.

Merrill, Thomas F. *Allen Ginsberg*, revised edition. Boston: Twayne Publishers, 1988.

Miles, Barry. *Allen Ginsberg—A Biography*. London: Virgin Books, 2000.

Packard, William. "Allen Ginsberg." *The Poet's Craft: Interviews From 'The New York Quarterly.'* " New York: Paragon, 1987: 30–51.

Parkinson, Thomas. "Reflections on Allen Ginsberg as a Poet." *Concerning Poetry*, 2 (1969): 21–24.

Perloff, Marjorie. "A Lion in Our Living Room: Reading Allen Ginsberg in the Eighties." *Poetic License: Essays On Modernist And Postmodernist Lyric*. Evanston, IL: Northwestern University Press (1990): 199–230.

Portuges, Paul. "Allen Ginsberg's Paul Cezanne and the *Pater Omnipotens Aeterna Deus*." *Comtemporary Literature* 21 (Summer 1980): 435–449.

Rodman, Selden. "Allen Ginsberg." *Tongues of Fallen Angels*. New York: New Directions, 1974: 183–199.

Rosenthal, M.L. "Allen Ginsberg." *The New Poets: American and British Poetry Since World War II*. New York: Oxford University Press, 1967: 89–112.

Schumacher, Michael. *Dharma Lion: A Critical Biography of Allen Ginsberg*. New York: St. Martins Press, 1994.

Trilling, Diana. "The Other Night at Columbia." *Partisan Review* 26 (Spring 1959): 214–230.

Tyaransen, Olaf. "And The Beat Goes On: An Interview with Allen Ginsberg." *Hot Press* (Winter/Spring 1995), vol. 19, no. 8. Available online at *http://iol.ie/hotpress/*.

WEBSITES

PAL: Perspectives in American Literature
www.csustan.edu/english/reuben/pal/chap10/ginsberg.html

Online Interviews with Allen Ginsberg
www.english.uiuc.edu/maps/poets/g_l/ginsberg/interviews.htm

Allen Ginsberg
www.naropa.edu/writingandpoetics/ginsberg.html

Allen Ginsberg.org Home
www.allenginsberg.org/home.asp

Allen Ginsberg: Life Stories, Books, & Links
www.todayinliterature.com/biography/allen.ginsberg.asp

INDEX

163

CONTRIBUTORS

NEIL HEIMS is a freelance writer, editor, and researcher. He has a Ph.D. in English from the City University of New York. He has written on a number of authors including Albert Camus, Arthur Miller, John Milton, and J.R.R. Tolkien.

LESLÉA NEWMAN is the author of 50 books including the picture books *Heather Has Two Mommies* and *The Boy Who Cried Fabulous;* the short story collections *A Letter to Harvey Milk* and *Out of the Closet and Nothing to Wear;* the poetry collection *Still Life with Buddy;* the novels *In Every Laugh a Tear* and *Jailbait;* and the writing manual, *Write from the Heart.* She has received many literary awards including Poetry Fellowships from the Massachusetts Artists Fellowship Foundation and the National Endowment for the Arts, the Highlights for Children Fiction Writing Award, the James Baldwin Award for Cultural Achievement, and three Pushcart Prize Nominations. Nine of her books have been Lambda Literary Award finalists.